THE
MOTHER AND DAUGHTER
PONY BOOK

Other Books Available

Exhibition and Practical Goatkeeping
Joan Shields

Book of the Netherland Dwarf
Denise Cumpsty

Exhibition and Pet Cavies
Isabel Turner

Fancy Goldfish Culture
Frank W. Orme

Famous Foxhunters
Daphne Moore

Exhibition and Pet Hamsters and Gerbils
Patricia Turner

THE MOTHER AND DAUGHTER PONY BOOK

by
JOAN SHIELDS

SAIGA PUBLISHING CO. LTD.,
1 Royal Parade,
Hindhead,
Surrey GU26 6TD, England.

© Joan Shields 1980
ISBN 0 904558 61 4

This book is copyright and may not be reproduced in whole *or in part* (except for a review) without the express permission of the publishers in writing.

Typeset by Inforum Ltd., Portsmouth
Printed and bound by
The Pitman Press, Bath

Published by
SAIGA PUBLISHING CO. LTD.,
1 Royal Parade,
Hindhead, Surrey GU26 6TD

Contents

Chapter		Page
Monochrome Illustrations List		vi
Acknowledgements		viii
1	May I Have a Pony?	1
2	General Management	13
3	The Paddock and the Shed	41
4	In the Saddle	47
5	Going to a Show	71
6	The Breeds	87
7	A Foal?	107
8	Societies and Clubs	113

Monochrome Illustrations

Figure		Page
Frontispiece: First — a wooden one		x
1.1	The points of a pony	4
1.2	A Mother-and-Daughter pony	8
1.3	Ideal ponies	10
1.4	The grooming kit	11
2.1	Pony at grass	14
2.2	Feeding	15
2.3	Feeding utensils	16
2.4	A variety of bits	19
2.5	Parts of a saddle	20
2.6	A well-fitting saddle	21
2.7	The bridle	22
2.8	Fetching a pony to be groomed	24–25
2.9	Grooming	28–29
2.10	Tacking-up	32–33
2.11	Some poisonous plants	35
3.1	The paddock	40
3.2	The shed	41
3.3	Adequate fencing is essential	43
4.1	Learning to ride	48
4.2	Mounting	51
4.3	Position of the foot in the stirrup	52
4.4	An example of a good seat	53

4.5	Holding the reins	54
4.6	Progressing from the 'walk' to the 'trot'	57
4.7	Using a lungeing rein	59
4.8	Jumping	60
4.9	Riding on the road	63
4.10	You can't catch me!	65
4.11	Leading your pony	67
5.1	Competing	70
5.2	All set!	76
5.3	Pony ready to compete in an In-hand class	78
5.4	Fun and games for all	79
5.5	Concentration	81
5.6	The smart pony	83
6.1	New Forest pony in his natural surroundings	86
6.2	New Forest pony	88
6.3	Highland stallion	90
6.4	Highland pony	91
6.5	Dartmoor ponies	93
6.6	Connemara pony	95
6.7	Welsh Mountain pony	97
6.8	Welsh pony yearling filly	99
6.9	Welsh cob	101
6.10	Dales pony	102
6.11	Exmoor winners	104
6.12	Fell pony	104
7.1	Two three-day old Welsh fillies	106
7.2	Mother and Daughter	109
7.3	Contentment	111
7.4	Welsh Colt foal	112
8.1	Pony Club meeting	114
8.2	At a Pony Club gymkhana	116
8.3	Fell ponies enacting 'The Border Reevers'	117

Acknowledgements

The Author is very grateful to all the breeders who have submitted beautiful photographs of Native ponies, to the Breed Societies and, in particular, to the National Pony Society, the parent body. At first glance it might appear that the Mother and Daughter (or Son, of course — but there are five little girls "horse-mazed" to every one little boy) might have their sights set too high by these lovely ponies. However, it is important to remember that a good Native pony probably costs less to keep than a mongrel, and a pretty pony with good conformation and breed type will give greater pleasure to work with; not to mention the pride of ownership which goes a long way to keeping the child's care of her mount up to scratch. Meg Mason's chapter on Showing may inspire both. So good luck to all the Mothers and Daughters who are about to take the plunge and buy that first pony.

Special thanks are offered to Mrs. Susan Hulme and her daughter, who were kind enough to pose for a number of photographs. These were required to illustrate important steps in the riding and management of ponies.

My thanks are also extended to the following for use of their photographs: Mrs. P. Blake, K.G. Ettridge, and Mrs. P. Fitzgerald, and to the undernoted photographers: Jane Miller, Charles Curtis and Len Petherbridge.

Frontispiece First – a wooden one

CHAPTER 1

May I Have a Pony?

MAKING A START

Sooner or later, but mostly sooner, Mother is asked "Can I have a pony?" To those for whom the horse is a large animal which kicks at one end and bites at the other, the thought fills them with consternation, but let them take heart for this book is for them.

There are many splendid books on horse management, on advanced horsemanship and, not forgetting the Pony Club Manuals, a wealth of reading and instruction for the child once she has attained the necessary standard to comprehend them. This book is not only a guide for the young rider as it is hoped that it will also help the Mother with the small child in her pre-Pony Club days, when Mother is perhaps also learning to ride and needs a simple reference book to help her to look after that first pony.

So, let both Mother and Daughter enjoy every minute of finding out about ponies, looking after them and riding them together.

AVOIDING THE SNAGS

Before saying "Yes", do consider what even a small pony will need, and whether you are able to provide it. If the child is small and light, it is unlikely that her first pony will carry her Mother too, for it may well be only 10 or 11 hands high, (signified by the letters h.h., and measured by the withers. A "hand" being 4 inches). An elderly pony, the beloved old friend of a growing-up family, is the ideal for it will not require daily exercise to keep it quiet enough for a beginner.

SHED

Even a small, quiet pony will need a shed in his paddock, open-fronted but a refuge from flies in summer and very bad weather. In the shed there should be a fresh bucket of water, a mineral lick brick and, when the grass is gone, a hay net kept filled.

COSTS

A guide to costs is given below. These are correct at the time of writing, but will obviously vary over a period.

HAY

If the paddock is over an acre, one pony will not need feeding with hay from May till October. His winter hay ration will be between 4 and 7 lb daily, so budget for half to one bale per week, at a cost of around 50p to £1.50, according to locality and season for hay-making.

SHOEING

The pony will need shoeing every six weeks, unless the family are lucky enough to live on the downs or on open moorland. This will cost something in the region of £6 to £7.50. A pony, little used, will still need his shoes removed and his hooves trimmed every six to eight weeks. This will cost about £5.

TACK

The pony's tack, saddle and bridle will cost about another £100 and the odds and ends, like saddle soap, grooming kit, hoof oil, buckets and so on will add up to another £10.

Having looked these bare essentials over, and having decided that keeping a pony is not altogether out of the question, what about the probable cost of the pony himself.

THE FIRST PONY

The first pony requires a perfect character, rather than perfect conformation, and in order to obtain this, together with soundness and good health, one must expect to pay; bearing in mind that one is paying for the safety of one's child. However, there are ways of cutting down upon this initial outlay which will be explained later. A sum of between £200 and £250 is suggested.

CLOTHING

The most important part of a child's riding clothing is her hard riding hat, without which she should never be allowed to mount. This should be of an approved, regulation type, and be secured by a chin strap or elastic. No matter how quiet the pony is, he may fall down, take fright, or roll in a nice puddle, and a hard hat which parts company with its wearer is of no use to anyone.

Never allow a child to ride in sand shoes. If jodhpur boots are too costly and too soon outgrown, let her wear stout brogues with leather heels. A small foot can all too easily slip right through the stirrup iron and become wedged, with fearful consequences if the rider falls and dangles. Apart from shoes and a hard hat, any good thick cotton jeans, jersey or shirt, together with an anorak for bad weather, will do for a start.

These, then, are the main expenses, and so we progress to the snags to be avoided when buying a pony.

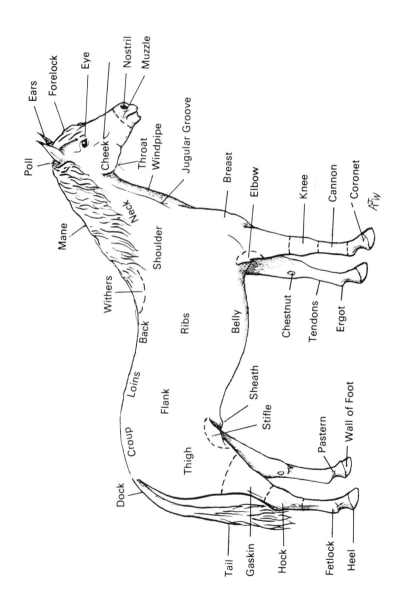

Fig. 1.1 The points of a pony.

THE IDEAL FIRST PONY

When choosing the first pony for one's child it is best to look for one which has enjoyed a happy situation with a knowledgeable family, but which has now been sadly outgrown. Ideally, the pony's first owners should have been brought up to respect and understand the needs of their pony and to put these needs before their own personal wishes. In short, the ideal first pony would be one which has never been asked to do anything unreasonable, and so happily responds to instructions. Where can this paragon be obtained? The following may be tried, in this order:

> The Secretary of the local Pony Club
> The farrier, or blacksmith
> The local newspaper
> The horse press (for example: *Horse & Hound, Riding, Pony World*).

In omitting the local dealer from the list, the Author is not in any way condemning him. He can be a very useful and helpful chap, but the outgrown family pony is unlikely to find his way to the dealer's yard for, as one of their dearest friends, the family will want to vet his new owner. It is often useful to ask the farrier if he knows of a suitable pony from any of his clients, for it is in this way that one can sometimes obtain a real bargain at a modest price by promising not to re-sell without the previous owner's knowledge.

If the Daughter is ten years old or more, then consider a pony which will be up to Mother's weight as well. The breeds of large Native pony are:

> The Highland
> The Dales
> The Fell
> The Welsh Cob
> The New Forest
> The Connemara

Even an Exmoor or a Dartmoor will carry a light adult hacking. (Refer to Chapter 6 for details of all the various breeds.)

DRIVING

All the Native breeds are suitable for driving, if this is envisaged as a pleasant and economical way of getting about. Naturally, though, one would expect to pay more for a ride-and-drive pony which was capable and had been trained in both jobs. A pony harness will cost upwards of £100 and a small, light vehicle about £165 to £600, according to type and condition.

AGE

A pony, with good management and some luck, will live to the ripe old age of twenty to thirty years. The first pony, as has been said, should not be a young one but middle-aged, as it is not good that both pony and child should be beginners. A ten year old pony is ideal, so it is a good idea to learn how one can tell the age of ponies by their teeth, for you may want to get a rough idea of this before going to the expense of having the pony vetted.

HEIGHT

Ponies start at about 10 h.h., the miniature Shetlands being even smaller. However, although small in height, most Shetlands are rather too wide for a tiny child and some are distinctly self-willed, so that to know the Shetland's history is necessary. From three years to ten years old, a child might be well suited with one of the small Native breeds; see Chapter 6 for details of these.

Once the size of the child comes within the scope of the larger Native breeds and their crosses, Mother may ride too, and it may well be that the pony which carried the twelve year old and her Mother may stay to carry her when she is a grown-up, married woman. One such pony is illustrated in Fig. 1.2.

Most small ponies will eventually be out-grown as the young rider shoots up, and then will come the sad day when they must be found good homes and a larger mount purchased to take their place. It is better if this fact is accepted from the start. The Author has had first hand experience of this "growing-out" of ponies and so, when helping friends to find the right pony for their children, tends to look for one which will last the ten or eleven year old indefinitely, as well as being up to Mother's weight. This kind of pony is probably no oil painting, and not a show one, but one which can give the whole family a lot of fun. Two examples of the ideal pony are as follows:

The Irish hunting pony probably contains some Irish Draught Horse blood and one of this sort, about 14.2 h.h., is illustrated (Fig. 1.3). These particular ponies may carry their owners from the age of eleven years onwards, and still carry them when they are grown up and married. The pony in question is hardy and lives out, but has access to her stable. Another cross-bred pony is illustrated (see Fig. 1.3), she is a first cross Welsh-New Forest pony of about 13.1 h.h. She would carry a child and a light adult.

The pure Native pony breeds are illustrated in a separate chapter, and it should be easy to come to a decision as to which is the most suitable. However, availability at the time is likely to play some part in the ultimate choice.

THE PURCHASE

Having decided to look at a prospective purchase, try to enlist the help of a knowledgeable friend, preferably one who will try the pony. Have the pony tacked up and brought out and watch how he responds to handling. He should be quiet, friendly, but interested. If he comes out of his stable in an orderly manner and stands like a rock to be mounted, then this is one good mark in his favour. He

Fig. 1.2 A Mother-and-Daughter pony
(*Photo courtesy:* Susan Hulme)

should walk away from home, turn towards home, and again turn away from home without any sign of unwillingness or argument. It is also wise to get the experienced friend to ride him far enough along the road to find out how he behaves in traffic. **If he is not one hundred per cent safe and free from nerves, don't buy him.**

Now ask to see him ridden in the field — will he canter quietly round without bucking? Does he have to be kicked along, continually breaking into a trot, or stopping? If he goes nicely and smoothly in both directions, then this is another good mark for him. When asked to halt and stand still, he should do just that and not be continually fidgeting and circling. In other words, a canter round the field should not make him "hot up".

Having satisfied yourself that the pony is the size, shape and character which you are looking for, call in your veterinary surgeon to vet him thoroughly, explaining that you do not know enough about horses to buy unaided. Ask him to tell you if the pony moves straight, has good legs and feet, is thoroughly sound and is likely to make a good mount for your beginner-child.

A well-known horsey character would probably ask for the pony on a week's trial, but as you cannot claim to be more than a novice, this would be unfair. Therefore, you will have to rely, firstly, upon your friend's judgement and, secondly, on the vet's report.

PREPARATION FOR THE ARRIVAL OF THE NEW PONY

Before the pony is due to arrive, check up that you have everything ready which is absolutely essential. The list below is really one of the bare essentials only, to which you may wish to add items as it becomes clear that they are needed:

Head collar and rope with clip-on end.

Fig. 1.3 Ideal ponies   *Top:* Irish Hunting Pony
Bottom: Welsh–New Forest Pony

Two hay nets; one in use and one to fill ready for replacing.
Feed pan and water bucket
Salt lick-brick (a large Rockie lasts a long time).
Saddle; with girth, leathers and irons. The latter not too small if Mother is riding as well.
Bridle
Two stable rubbers
Two sponges: one for dock and one for eyes.
Rubber Curry Comb
Dandy Brush
Body Brush
Hoof Pick
Mane Comb
Tail Bandage
Flexalan or similar leather dressing
Saddle Soap

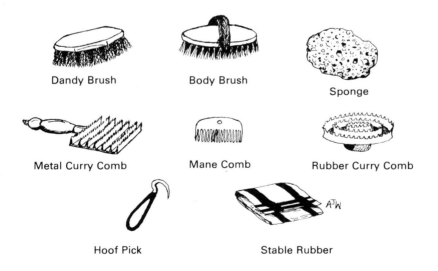

Fig. 1.4 The grooming kit.
If your pony is to be properly cared for, the above will be essential.

Brush for applying oil to tack
Sponge for use with Saddle Soap
Hoof Oil and Brush for applying
A small quantity of Pony Nuts; these are really to catch the pony, and to have a handful in his pan ready for him when he is brought in, (see Chapter on Feeding).
Hay: a year's requirement is probably around 1 ton, but this is usually bought by the bale.
Bran: preferably Broad Bran — not easy to get now. About ½ cwt. will be needed.

CHAPTER 2

General Management

FEEDING PONIES

Without knowledge of the prevailing circumstances and the size and work to be done by the pony, it is not possible to lay down any exact rules as to his feeding. Instead, we must take two or three examples of ponies differing in size and then other ponies can be judged by the nearest example to their own.

Beginning with a 10 h.h. small child's leading-rein pony, little else will be required but good grass in summer and hay in winter. The amount will of course depend on the appetite of the particular pony but he will also need a mineral lick-brick and clean water.

A 12.2 H.H. PONY

The 12.2 h.h. pony, carrying an average eleven year old, may be used for regular hacking and for some Pony Club activities. Apart from the basic diet outlined above, he will also require some pony nuts. These are suitable because they are a low protein, high fibre food and, in consequence, will nourish the pony without hotting him up as plain oats would do.

Two feeds a day in summer, when out at grass, is sufficient and the suggested amount for this 12.2 h.h. pony when

Fig. 2.1 Pony at Grass.

GENERAL MANAGEMENT

doing some work is 2 lb of pony nuts plus 1 lb of damped broad bran. The pony should be fed two hours before exercise in the morning; the same rule applying to his evening feed.

During the winter the pony may be used for hunting once a week for a few hours and he will, therefore, require an extra nightly feed during the hunting season. For this feed the pony may be given a small amount of well-scalded sugar beet pulp or, as an alternative, about 2 lb of diced carrot.

Whether the beet pulp comes in nut form or in shreds, it **must** be soaked in boiling water and left for twelve hours before feeding. Horses, not being ruminants like cattle, cannot cope with any food which swells inside them. One has only to see how soon a half-filled bucket of beet pulp becomes brim-full to visualize what might happen to the stomach of an unfortunate pony! The amount to soak,

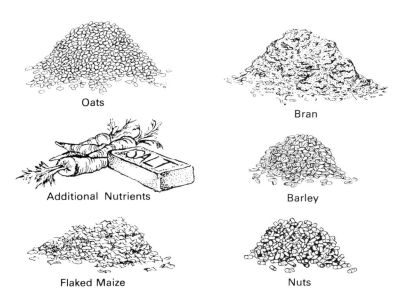

Fig. 2.2 Feeding – a balanced and varied diet, using any of the above foods, will help to keep your pony healthy and happy.

weighed dry, is 4 — 6 oz for a 12.2 h.h. pony. Before feeding, the pulp should be dried off with a scoopful of broad bran, and a teaspoon of salt should be added.

Grass nuts may also be given but, as there is already dried grass meal in the pony nuts, they are best used as an alternative rather than as an addition to the basic winter diet. With this size of pony the hay-net will normally need replenishing three times daily.

A 14 H.H. PONY

For the larger Mother-and-Daughter type of mount, which will be about 14 h.h., we might well study the diet sheet of the Author's own ponies: a pure Highland of 13.3 h.h. and a half Highland/half Thoroughbred pony of about 14.3 h.h.

In the summer the former is given 1 lb of damp broad bran together with a single handful of pony nuts in the

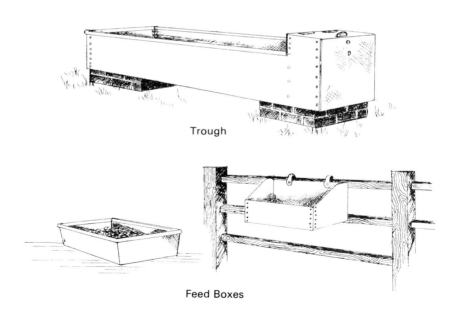

Trough

Feed Boxes

Fig. 2.3 Feeding utensils

morning. This is given merely as a token feed since he is ridden only two or three times weekly, and then only at a slow pace. This feed is repeated in the evening. The latter, who is a growing filly, has about 1 lb of **stud** nuts with about 2 lb of damp broad bran.

It is important that the ponies should come when called, and that they are not made jealous of each other's feeds. To prevent this they are fed separately in the stables twice daily. If only one stable is available, one pony should be fed outside the door.

By October the goodness has largely gone out of the grass. Therefore, good hay should be provided in nets, preferably hung from trees in the ponies' field or paddock and well out of reach of the ponies' feet. This hay then serves as a supplement to the normal, twice-daily feed.

By November, the ponies will be ready for a feed of about 2 lb of diced carrots or swedes. This should be given at around 4 — 5 p.m. when, by this time of year, it will be dark. At 8 p.m. they should be given a feed of soaked beet pulp, together with broad bran. The hay nets should be re-filled and this time hung in the stable; the stable doors being opened after feeding so that they may come and go at will. By December the stables should be bedded down with good thick straw or shavings, as available, and on wet and wintery nights ponies will usually be found lying comfortably asleep inside their stables. However, they should not be shut in and very often will be found grazing at the crack of dawn before their owner is about. This arrangement will give a pony a feeling of security and comfort, but of course one could not follow out this plan with two or more ponies who were not already firm friends.

AN "IN–FOAL" MARE

Turning to Chapter 7, in which we consider the possibility of breeding a foal, the feeding of a little mare will need to be increased during November, December and the early spring months. The mare will need about 4 lb of stud nuts, according to her size, together with some damp broad bran, in two feeds daily. The mid-day feed may consist of diced carrots, and the hot beet pulp feed may well be given last thing at night. **"Little and often" should be the rule for in-foal mares.**

It is important that the in-foal mare has all the vital minerals, vitamins and other necessary nutrients. These are contained in the stud nuts, but if the grazing is good and the amount of stud nuts required is, therefore, small, Equivite may be added to the feed to ensure that the right vitamins and minerals are supplied.

The diet of any pony will depend much upon the quality and area of the grazing land. Therefore, no hard and fast rules as to the required amounts of other feed can be laid down. This chapter is intended as a guide to the basic diet required by the average pony. However, the needs and requirements of one's own pony must never be ignored for the sake of adhering to text-book rules.

FITTING AND CARING FOR THE PONY'S SADDLE AND BRIDLE

The saddle and bridle, called **tack**, are expensive items and can be very difficult to replace if they are, as we hope, a perfect fit for both you and your pony. Therefore, if the pony's previous owner has his tack available for sale, look it over carefully to make sure that it is sound and really fits the pony, as well as both you and your child. If this can be managed then it will be a good investment. The fact that tack may suit both Mother and Daughter may sound impossible but this is not so; the saddle may be one size too big for the daughter and yet still give good service.

There are Pony Club approved saddles of a pattern which is excellent for general purposes, and which are very comfortable. If you have to buy a new saddle go to a

GENERAL MANAGEMENT

reputable saddler and ask to see one of these, telling him the height and type, or breed, of your pony.

FITTING

In the good old days one rode one's horse to the saddler, whereupon he emerged and took note of the mount's requirements and of your own, and in due course turned out a saddle to fit both; if he had none in stock. The Author bought a good second-hand Souter hunting saddle for £2.00 in this way. Your pony's saddle will now cost as much as the pony himself cost in those days.

Take the fit of the bridle first; this will probably be a snaffle with a wide mouth piece and an ordinary nose band, as shown in Fig. 2.4. This also shows a Kimblewick bit which is suitable for an older child with a pony which needs greater control. There are many other combinations of nose bands and bits, but these two are the most suitable for a well-behaved, well-schooled pony with a young rider.

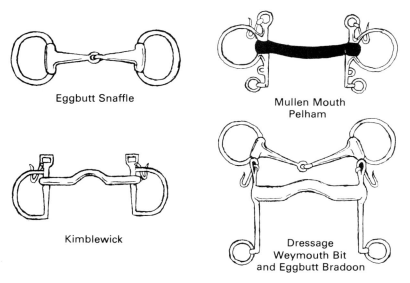

Fig. 2.4 A variety of bits – the two on the left are most suitable for a well-balanced pony with a young rider.

Before fitting the bridle, each piece should be seen separately.

Five points to follow when fitting a bridle

Once the bridle has been put together and is ready to fit the following should be taken into account:

1. The brown band must not be too tight, thereby restricting the movement of the pony's ears.
2. The nose band should be fitted so that it lays just below the cheek bones. It should be buckled loosely enough to enable three fingers to be inserted between the band and the underneath of the jaw.
3. The cheek pieces should be buckled to the bit so that the bit barely wrinkles the sides of the mouth. The bit itself should extend about 1/3 of an inch at each side of the mouth.
4. The throat lash should be fastened loosely enough to

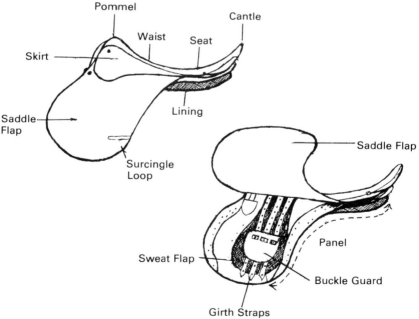

Fig. 2.5 Parts of a saddle.

GENERAL MANAGEMENT

enable a couple of fingers to be inserted under it, and if a curb chain is used this must be turned and turned until the links lie flat. One extra turn should then be given in the same direction before it is hooked onto the second side. **The curb chain must lie flat in the groove of the pony's chin.**

5. The reins may be of plain leather, plaited leather or nylon.

Five points to follow when fitting a sadle

The vital points to take into account when fitting a saddle are as follows:

1. There must be a clear passage of air and light through the channel running down the back from the pommel to the cantle.
2. You should be able to put three fingers between the

Fig. 2.6 A well-fitting saddle.

pommel and the withers, when mounted.
3. You should be able to sit well down in the saddle without feeling either that you are falling backwards, or having to cling on.
4. The panels of the saddle should be soft and supple; you should be able to feel the pony through them; your legs should not be pushed away from the pony's sides by an immense amount of stuffing.
5. The girth straps are, of course, a vital part of the saddle, as are the leathers. These should be carefully checked to ensure that they are sound, especially on a second-hand saddle. Ideally, the saddle should be taken in every year for re-stuffing if needed, and a general overhaul.

It is also important to note that at any time a mark or rubbed area is noticed on the pony when the saddle is removed, the corresponding point on the saddle itself

Fig. 2.7 The bridle – it is important that this kept clean and supple.
(*Photo courtesy:* Susan Hulme)

should be checked, for there may be a thorn, twig, or a rough hard spot on it.

CLEANING THE SADDLE AND BRIDLE

Once a week the saddle and bridle should be dismantled in order that they may be cleaned thoroughly. It is best to take a careful note, before dismantling, of which holes the various buckles were done up to and, if the child is to do the cleaning, these should be checked afterwards to ensure that they are correct before being used.

Both saddle and bridle should be washed thoroughly using saddle soap and warm water. **Hot water should never be used**. All sweat and mud should be sponged from the bridle, girths, and underside of the saddle. They should then be left to dry naturally; never before a fire. Once they are dry, **Flexalan** oil dressing should be applied to the underside of the saddle, the girth straps, the buckle guard and the underside of the panels. Once this oil has soaked in, saddle soap may be applied very sparingly to the upper parts of the saddle and wiped over with a clean, soft cloth. The bridle should receive a thorough soaping, and also the reins if they are made of leather. Flexalan may also be applied to the bridle, if it has become harsh and stiff. If the reins are made of nylon, they may be washed along with any nylon girths; leather girths should be unfolded and the three sides well dressed with oil. If there is a flannel strip running the length of the girth, this may be soaked in oil in order to keep the girth supple. The stirrup irons and bit should also be thoroughly washed and then polished with long-term silver polish, but don't forget to wash off the rather horrid taste it may leave off of the bit!

When re-assembling the tack, the leathers should be put back on the same side as before, as they then tend to swing in the right direction and lie flat along the rider's leg. It is then easier for you to find the irons at once with your toes. The leathers should be checked to see that they have

Step 1
Whilst holding the head collar behind you, call your pony and entice him with a titbit.

Step 2
Once he is eating from your hand, stand at the side of his head, making sure that you still keep his head collar behind you.

Fig. 2.8 Fetching a pony to be groomed.
(*Photos courtesy:* Susan Hulme)

Step 3
Slowly slip the head collar rope round his neck. Keep all your movements slow, gentle but deliberate.

Step 4
Next, put on the head collar and you may then lead him to be groomed.

Fig. 2.8 Fetching a pony to be groomed (cont.)
(*Photos courtesy:* Susan Hulme)

stretched evenly, because this is not always the case and correspondingly numbered holes are not necessarily a guarantee that they are level.

Particularly in winter, when the pony's back is naturally greasy — to keep out the cold and wet — it helps if an old stable rubber or tea cloth is put under the saddle in order to keep it clean. However, the cloth must be pulled up into the pommel, so that the channel is not restricted by it.

It is as well to note that a wooden saddle-horse is useful for leaving or for cleaning the saddle on, but if you have to stand it down, always stand it on end.

GROOMING

FETCHING A PONY

Fetching the pony from his field and getting him ready for riding should not take many minutes. Any problems must be solved at the very beginning for he must be thoroughly cleaned, particularly in winter, if he lives out, and no part of the work involved can be ignored just because there are difficulties.

Firstly, put a few pony nuts in his pan inside his shed, or wherever else you decide that you will always tie him in order to groom and saddle-up. Secondly, take his head collar, with the rope, and a titbit to entice him to you. Do not go right up to him, but call him and let him come the last few yards to you. Whilst doing this, you should hold the head collar behind you.

Haltering

Once he is close to you, stand at the side of his neck and quietly slip the halter, or head collar rope, round his neck and then put the head collar on. If he is new and does not come readily to call, it is best to leave the head collar on at all times until he accepts you. However, always take and attach the rope, in order that he may be led. Whilst telling him to walk on, lead him on at a level with his shoulder and tie him up wherever you decide that you will always groom him.

HOOF-PICKING

Firstly, pick out his feet, starting with the inside fore foot. Face his tail and run your hand down the back of his leg whilst saying "Up". Clean the hoof from the heel towards the toe, taking particular care round the frog which is the triangular part. Now pick up the hind foot on the same side, after running your hand down the pony's quarters, and bring it backwards until it rests on your knee. **Do not pull it out sideways** as the joint does not work in that direction, and the Author once had a pony lamed in this way by an apprentice-farrier.

When cleaning out the pony's feet each day before riding, you should take note of the state of his shoes so that if there is a nail missing, or the shoe is worn down unevenly and pressing into the foot at the heel, it will be noticed right away. This means that the blacksmith may then be booked for an appointment before the problem becomes serious. These gentlemen are hard to come by in a hurry, and clearly the pony must not work if his shoes are not in order.

GROOMING THE COAT

Starting at the neck, brush the pony down, using the **Dandy brush** in winter or the **Body brush** if he has his summer coat. Clean the brush on the **Curry comb** every few strokes and tap the curry on the floor to remove the dust. Always use the Body brush on his head, which should be brushed gently and with care. Some ponies are "head shy" because they have been roughly handled at some time in their lives and their eyes have been damaged or hurt.

Mane, Tail and Eyes

The next step is to groom the mane and tail which must

Step 1
Firstly, pick out your pony's feet using a hoof pick. Take special care when lifting his leg and when cleaning around the frog.

Step 2
When grooming the coat, ensure that you clean the brush on the Curry comb every few strokes.

(*Photo courtesy:* Susan Hulme)

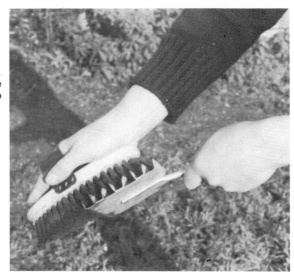

Fig. 2.9 Grooming.

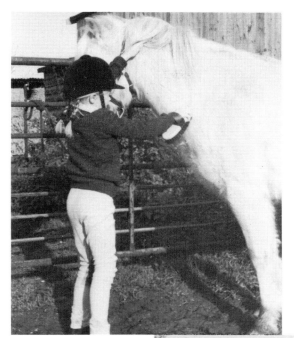

Step 3
Brush your pony down, starting at the neck. Always take especial care when brushing his head and always use the Body brush on this area.

Step 4
Thoroughly brush and comb his mane and tail, but be gentle and stand to one side whilst doing so.

Fig. 2.9 Grooming (cont.)
(*Photos courtesy:* Susan Hulme)

be thoroughly brushed and combed. His eyes and dock (underpart of tail) should be sponged using a separate sponge for each.

HOOVES

Lastly, his hooves should be oiled using a brush and hoof oil. In very dry weather, this latter part of grooming becomes very important and, although oiled hooves look nicer, it is not of such importance to oil them when they are damp. **Hooves must always be oiled after the pony has been shod.**

The pony's feet may have a tendency to "ball up" in the snow. In order to prevent this, try larding round the frog and the inside of the shoe. Engine oil may be used as an alternative.

TACKING-UP

Once he has been groomed, the pony is ready for his saddle and bridle. Take the bridle in one hand, with the reins and headpiece together, and place the saddle over the other arm with the pommel nearest to you. Talk to the pony whilst running a hand down his back and tell him to "get over" until he is in the required position. If, at any time, you must put the saddle down, make sure that it is the pommel end which is on the ground. Once the pony is standing still, slip the reins over his neck and remove the head collar. Than stand beside him, facing the same way that he is, and put your right hand round and up to take the bridle head, whilst using your left to insert the bit very gently, but firmly, into his mouth. Let all your actions be firm, gentle, but deliberate. Nothing makes a pony fidget quicker than a fiddling groom. Do up the nose band, throat lash and put on the saddle and take note of the points layed out on p. 21–22. Once the pony is tacked up, he is ready to be ridden. It is imperative to remember to slip the reins over the pony's head when leading him through gates or out of doors and always, when leading out of the stable, keep the irons run up the leathers.

AVOIDING THE DANGERS

Very few ponies are so unpleasant in character that they will kick or bite without any reason; the horse's first line of defence is flight. If the pony **knows** that you are going to pick out his feet, walk round his back-side, or slap a saddle on his back, then these actions will become part of the normal day's events and will be accepted as such. If, however, your actions are sudden and unexpected he may take fright and a nervous horse, like a nervous dog, is unpredictable.

If a pony has a tendency to kick it is best if you keep as near to his quarters as you possibly can when moving round him. Then you will not receive the full force of the kick. The kick which hurts is that which just reaches you with the full force at the full extent of the leg. Ponies seldom "cow-kick"; that is, kick sideways. A snappy pony must be tied up for grooming as some reach round and bite when girthed up, particularly mares. It is to be hoped that this type of pony has not come your way, but if it does, meet that open mouth with a good stiff-bristled Dandy brush as it swings round to grab!

Perhaps the Author has been lucky (or wise in choice), but only one unpleasant pony has come her way in sixty years with horses. This one, a good pony when sane, had a brain tumour and so was not responsible for her actions when she appeared to go berserk.

Most ponies love being groomed and every little attention is regarded with obvious pleasure. Human companionship is extremely important to lone ponies who have no friend of their own species to graze with. However, it is important to remember, when keeping more than one

Step 1
Mother shows the way. Stand beside your pony and put your right hand round and up to take the bridle head. Use your left hand to insert the bit gently, but firmly into his mouth.

Step 2
Next, do up the nose and throat bands whilst taking note of all the important points layed out on page 20.

Fig. 2.10 Tacking-up.

(*Photos courtesy:* Susan Hulme)

Step 3
Once your pony is tacked-up and ready to be ridden you may lead him out of his paddock. Always keep a firm hold on the leading rain and lead him on a level with his shoulders. Do not drag him behind you.

Step 4
When leading your pony, make sure that the irons are run up the leathers.

Fig. 2.10 Tacking-up (cont.)

(*Photos courtesy:* Susan Hulme)

pony, that the definition of "horseplay" really means rough stuff, and two ponies who are really great friends may be enjoying such a rough game that to get near them at the time would be stupid. Children should certainly be warned to watch out and avoid coming between them.

AILMENTS: THEIR PREVENTION AND TREATMENT

Ponies at grass, who are sensibly managed, very seldom suffer from any illness, but because prevention is always better than cure it is hoped that you will read this section before any illness arises. There will be no feverish turning of the pages if you have read and understood the following, as you will know what to do. You should also know whether to call in the veterinary surgeon without delay.

The list of common illnesses is not an alarming one, but nevertheless it is important that any symptoms are quickly spotted so that correct treatment may be speedily given. Here follows a list of the most common ailments, their symptoms and treatment.

COLIC

Colic is really a symptom rather than a disease, but as it can prove fatal if not quickly and correctly treated, the layman must watch for the first signs of disorder.

Symptoms

An intermittent pain, causing the pony to look at its stomach, sweat and have an anxious expression. The pony will then begin lying down and rising again, walking round in circles and rolling on the ground. His breathing will be hard and laboured, whilst his pulse will be fast.

Cure

The first step in righting this disorder is to telephone

GENERAL MANAGEMENT

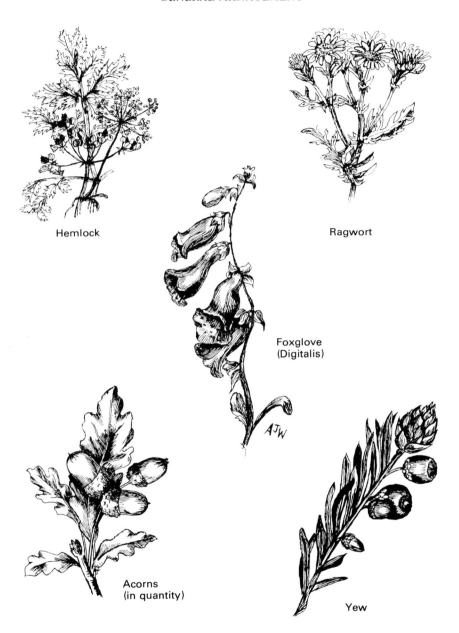

Fig. 2.11 Some poisonous plants.
Your pony should never be allowed to eat any of the above.

your vet and tell him that you have a case of colic. He will probably give the pony an injection to ease the tension in the stomach and a drench (dose) of linseed oil, medicinal turpentine and ground ginger. Olive oil may be substituted for the linseed and whisky may also be added. In the event of the vet being unobtainable through, for example, extremely hazardous road conditions, a drench could be made and administered for a 12 h.h. pony, as follows:

- 1 tablespoonful medicinal turpentine
- 2 tablespoonfuls whisky
- $\frac{1}{2}$ teaspoonful ground ginger
- $\frac{1}{2}$ pint olive oil

Repeat dose in three hours if necessary, halving the turpentine.

Causes

Causes are: acute indigestion, various disorders of the stomach and bowel, heavy infestation of parasitic worms, bots, etc., over-feeding and cold water being given when the pony is over-heated after exercise.

Prevention

Prevention consists of keeping a steady varied diet; feeding small quantities regularly; making no sudden changes to the diet; giving stabled horses some succulents, for example: carrots, swedes, apples and mangolds. Dusty or musty hay must be avoided.

Water must always be given before meals. If the pony has been hunting, or to a Pony Club outing, water with the chill off should be offered before feeding but not a great amount. Most Native ponies seem to know that they must not drink much when hot and tired and will just dabble their mouths in the water.

LAMINITIS

Below the outer horny wall of the foot there is a sensitive laminae which, for reasons not yet fully understood, becomes inflamed and swollen thereby causing great pain and often lameness as the pressure from the swelling increases.

Symptoms

The pony may become lame in one or more feet and will resist all efforts directed towards making him move. He may also lie down frequently to ease the pain and show fear of having the foot tapped or pressed. After some time rings may appear around the hoof.

Cure

Applications of a cold water hose to the legs and feet two or three times daily may be a help or, in chronic cases, a special shoe fitted by the farrier is, perhaps, the best answer.

Causes

Causes of laminitis are somewhat obscure. Treatment with antihistamine has sometimes been effective, so that in some ponies the possibility of an allergy being the main cause cannot be ruled out.

Prevention

It is essential to keep the diet simple, withholding oats and other heating foods whilst concentrating on the use of hay and greenstuff. However, rich, young grass pasture should be avoided. Ponies with a tendency to laminitis should be removed from this type of pasture, especially when the grass protein is at its highest – from May to July.

SWEET ITCH

This is an old name for a type of eczema in ponies which is thought to result from an allergic reaction to the bite of a certain midge. Sweet Itch, like laminitis is sometimes thought to occur when ponies are set to graze on rich summer pasture and although the true cause is not known, it is said that ponies affected by this ailment will benefit from being kept inside during the heat of the day.

SPLINTS

A splint is not a serious ailment, usually being callous by the time the animal is six years old. The only time a splint may cause problems is when one occurs in such a place as to interfere with the natural movement of the ligaments. Very few big horses are free from splints; they are seldom large enough to be seen but usually can be felt.

Symptoms

The pony can be seen to be lame when trotting but may often walk soundly.

Cure

It may be possible, with the use of an ointment supplied by the vet, to reduce the growth before it becomes callous. However, as has been said, prevention is better than cure.

Cause

Splints are usually caused by concussion of the pony's legs and feet upon hard ground, tarred roads or other surfaces of this nature.

Prevention

Young horses and ponies should be taken slowly on roads or hard ground and should never be taken beyond a slow trot. This rule also applies when there is either a drought or very frosty ground.

COLDS AND COUGHS

This ailment, when encountered in a pony, requires much the same treatment as it does in humans. The pony should be kept warm and out of draughts, but have access to plenty of fresh air. Light, nourishing foods should be given and also gentle exercise, unless he has a temperature.

THE MEDICINE CHEST

Medical requirements likely to be needed for ponies at grass are few because, as has already been said, they should remain healthy and sound if commonsense management is employed at all times and fields checked regularly for snags. The following, however, should always be readily available:

1. For colic (if no veterinary surgeon is immediately at one's disposal): colic drench, made up by the vet.
2. Terramycine spray for cuts, foot troubles and other disorders of this nature.
3. Epsom Salts.
4. Animal Lintex poultice (instructions are to be found on the packet).
5. 2 inch bandages (crepe) to cover poultice.
6. Worm powder: dose as and when advised by veterinary surgeon.

Whenever in doubt it is always best to call the vet.

Fig. 3.1 The paddock.
(*Courtesy*: Mrs P. Blake, *photo courtesy*: Jane Miller)

CHAPTER 3

The Paddock and the Shed

It is not advisable for a pony to be stabled unless he is doing fast, regular work. He will be happier, live longer and encounter less illness if he is kept in a paddock. However, he should have access to an open fronted shelter at all times. It will be found that he uses this shelter far more in the summer when the flies are troublesome, than in the winter when the weather is bad.

Fig. 3.2 The shed.

(*Courtesy*: Mrs P. Blake, *photo courtesy*: Jane Miller)

THE SHED

The size of shed required for a 12 h.h. pony is approximately 12 × 12 feet (3.66 × 3.66m). It must be high enough for the pony to stand upright at the rear of the building. Bedding is not always necessary but a good sand or chalk floor, kept clean, will be an asset.

The furnishings will simply consist of the pony's water bucket, hay net (in winter) and his mineral lick-brick. This shed will become his refuge, in time, and he will begin to feel secure here and be used to being led inside for grooming and saddling.

THE PADDOCK

The paddock must not be less than 1 acre and, if larger, is best divided with a single strand of electric fencing. By doing this, a change of scenery and grass may be given by using each half alternately. A 3 or 4 acre paddock may be divided into four and one quarter shut off for hay in April, to be cut during the first dry spell in June or July.

COMPANY

Horses are gregarious by nature and love to have a companion. If the pony will stay in his paddock alone, all well and good. However, if he will not a donkey, goat or even a goose may help, but beware of tethering a goat in a field with several ponies. The ponies attitude on this matter is an important point to enquire about when buying.

If there is a neighbour who also has a pony, it is a good idea to utilize one paddock for the two and then rest that paddock and use the other. A regular worm dose must be used on both ponies so that the land does not become "horse sick" because of a multitude of worms. The ponies will be happier together and will also benefit from the change of grass. The only snag to be encountered with the above idea lies in the fact that one pony may object to the other being taken away to be ridden. This must, therefore, be done tactfully at first, until the second pony accepts the fact that this loneliness is of very short duration. The Author solved this problem by giving a feed to the second pony, staying around for the first two or three times he was left and talking over the fence whilst gardening or such like, to keep him company.

THE POSSESSIVE PONY

Many children have to ride in the field which the pony considers his own personal property, and this is often resented. He may show a degree of unwillingness to co-operate, or even exhibit downright naughtiness. To prevent this, always try to arrange to ride in a different field if humanly possible, but not one which is next to where a second pony is grazing.

Fig. 3.3 Adequate fencing is essential – an example of good fencing.
(*Courtesy*: Mrs P. Blake, *photo courtesy*: Jane Miller)

It is always wise to remember that psychology is very much more important with little ponies than with big horses, for ponies think quickly and are extremely enterprising.

MANAGEMENT OF THE PONY AT GRASS

Whether ridden or not, ponies at grass must be visited at least twice daily to check that all is well. The water supply must be seen to, the fencing checked and the pony's feet picked out to make sure that there are no stones wedged between the frog (the triangular part) and the sole.

People living in urban areas will also need to make sure that no unsuitable offering has been thrown over the hedge or fence and into a pony's field. The Author has seen bottles, plastic bags, half-opened tins, bits of barbed wire, poisonous shrub trimmings and much other dangerous material being thrown into the pony's field. Ponies have also been lamed by hooligans breaking in and galloping the ponies around bareback.

When being used by a learner rider, the pony will not be expected to go very fast. Therefore, he may be haltered and led to his shed to be groomed and saddled before the lesson. However, when the young rider is off the leading rein, it is better for the pony if he is brought inside for an hour or two before being ridden so that he is not so full of grass. The pony may be tied up in the shed or to a couple of rails fitted to the shed front.

LIGHT FEEDS

Always have a **few** pony or grass nuts in the pony's pan so that he is pleased to come inside the shed in order to reach them. His water bucket should be kept full of fresh, clean water and, except in spring and summer, his hay net should be filled with sweet, free-from-dust hay.

THE PADDOCK AND THE SHED

Do not be tempted to feed oats when in the early stages of learning to ride, as these may well go to the pony's head and make an otherwise docile mount behave like a lunatic. **Oats may only be fed when a pony is doing enough work to need them**. The pony at grass in the winter is best fed ample hay, an occasional bran mash or a little well-scalded sugar beet pulp.

ATTENTION AFTER RIDING

After returning from a ride you should rub round your pony's ears and tummy where the girth straps have been, either using your hand or with wisps of hay. His feet should again be picked out and then he may be turned out into his field to roll. Never leave him tied up in the shed if he is hot as he may break out into a cold sweat. If this happens he will be much better off walking and grazing in his field. He may cover himself in mud as this will serve to keep him warm.

If his drinking water is kept in the shed it will not become chilled. Serving unchilled water is always a wise precaution, but the warning not to feed a hot pony and then give him ice cold water does not really concern us at this stage; he will not be ridden in the manner which would make him too hot.

GROOMING OF A PONY AT GRASS

Resist the temptation to brush your pony like mad to make him look lovely and shiny. When out at grass only the mud should be removed — particular care and attention should be taken over those parts which are covered when the pony is tacked up, for example: under the saddle and girths. The mane and tail may be brushed out, but on no account should the hair growing around his heels in the winter months be clipped. This is as essential as the natural grease on his skin and is there as a form of protection. His hooves, however, should be picked out regularly.

TIT-BITS

The Author feels that a word of warning about the feeding of tit-bits to ponies in paddocks should be included here. All children should know that, when going to catch and halter a pony, only a crust, two or three nuts or a carrot should be taken and nothing given at any other time. Some ponies may become very unpleasant and may turn round and kick out if the expected tit-bit fails to materialize. This can become even more unpleasant if more than one pony lives in the field as jealousy is a great cause of bad temper. To be caught in the cross-fire of two sets of kicking, iron-shod hooves is terrifying for a small child and is also extremely dangerous.

This is the reason for the **"Do Not Feed The Ponies"** notices in our National Parks, and one only wishes that visitors would comply, as feeding the ponies also encourages them onto the roads where dozens are killed every year.

CHAPTER 4

In the Saddle

LEARNING TO RIDE

When first learning to ride, there are three separate things to think about; the **pony**, its **saddle** and its **bridle**. Dealing with all three at once is really too much to grasp in one lesson and it is most important that you should not feel inadequate or nervous, and that every minute of the first lesson should be enjoyed. The lessons should not last too long, perhaps ten minutes the first day, increasing to half-an-hour as your muscles adjust to the new positions and movements.

LESSON ONE

Mother should supervise these first few lessons and the following directions are for her to follow.

Mounting

To start with, put only a neck strap on the pony. Any soft wide leather strap which will reach round the pony's neck will do. He should also be wearing a head collar or a snaffle bridle, whichever he leads best in, with a long rein. A large solid block of wood, if no mounting block is available, will help the young rider to mount; this method is better than just lifting her or giving her a leg up. Let her stand on the block and take the neck rein strap in her left hand, then she

Step 1
Mother should be at hand at all times to steady the rider as she mounts the pony.

Step 2
Once sitting comfortably she should be encouraged to exercise whilst in the saddle. Soon both pony and rider will be at ease with each other.

Fig. 4.1 Learning to ride

(*Photos courtesy:* Susan Hulme)

should throw her right leg across the pony's back. See that she is sitting comfortably and is holding the neck strap with both hands, then lead the pony forward saying "Walk on". Walk the pony a few paces round the yard, or up the drive, then halt and let the child lean back along the pony's back, sit up again, touch her right toe with her left hand and her left toe with her right hand. She should now be beginning to feel at home on him and will soon start to play on her own initiative probably swinging her legs over so that she is sitting facing his tail. This relaxation is to be encouraged, providing that the pony is a proper child's first pony and has experienced the very young learning to ride before. At no time should Mother let go of the leading rein, and she must always be ready with the other hand to right a sliding child.

Dismounting

Learning to dismount will complete the first lesson. Have the child holding onto the neck strap with her left hand. She should then kick both feet out of the stirrups and throw her right leg over the pony's back, thus sliding down onto her feet. A very small child will need holding until she is touching the ground with both feet. She should mount and dismount on the pony's left side; that is to say, the side which is on the left when one is facing his head. After the lesson the pony should be given a reward; for example, a small piece of carrot or apple. Then, together, Mother and Daughter should lead the pony back to his field. Once inside, he should be turned to face you before his head collar or bridle is taken off. This will prevent him getting into a habit of rushing off. A small child should never be allowed to lead a strong pony until the two are well acquainted and it is clear that a partnership exists. Ponies are very quick to take advantage and break away, and this is the last thing we want to happen.

LESSON TWO

Lesson Two may be a repeat of Lesson One, but very much will depend upon the age and temperament of the child. She may be quite content to be led around bareback or she may demand a saddle, but in no circumstances should she be allowed to use the bridle until she has become used to her saddle and is sitting correctly. Therefore, the neck-strap should be kept on for a while.

Using the Saddle

The stirrup irons should have been run up the leather and the girth thrown across the seat of the saddle. Place the saddle rather too high up on the pony's back and then slide it gently down a little until it settles naturally. The girth, which is always fastened to the off-side straps, should now be dropped and fastened under the pony's tummy, making sure that there are no twists in it. The buckles should be fastened fairly loosely to start with, as they are then pulled up a hole or two before mounting the child, and again when she is seated. The reason for this is that most ponies blow out their tummies when being girthed. **The girth should not be tightened up in one movement.**

Leave the irons run up the leathers when going through doors or gateways and until the child is ready to mount. They will not then bang about or get caught up, which must be explained to the child.

Let the child mount from the block as before but this time using the stirrups. A handful of mane should be taken in the left hand and the leathers given one turn away. She should then place her foot in the stirrup and, holding the back of the saddle with her right hand to steady her, she should be able to spring up onto the pony's back. Once mounted she should position her feet in the irons so that her toes are resting on the bar. Stand in front of the pony to see that the child is level, and then at her side to make sure that the length of the leather is correct. At this stage, the

Mounting the wrong way

Mounting the right way

Fig. 4.2 Mounting – Mother should watch carefully to see that the young rider mounts correctly and also should keep the pony steady.

body should only just clear the saddle when standing up in the stirrups. The young rider should, after her exercises without the saddle, be sitting down in the saddle as if still riding bareback but now with her feet directly under her body in the stirrups, and with the toes turning inwards, (see Fig. 4.3).

After being led around the yard a few times she will become used to her position in the saddle and may then progress to Lesson Three.

LESSON THREE

The pony should be fully tacked up with both saddle and bridle and the child should mount as before only this time the reins should be held in the left hand as she is mounting, as well as a handful of mane.

Fig. 4.3 Position of the feet in the stirrup.

(*Photo courtesy:* Susan Hulme)

Fig. 4.4 An example of a good seat.
Note that the child is sitting down in the saddle, with her legs and feet directly under her body and with the toes turned inwards.

(*Photo courtesy:* Susan Hulme)

Using the Bridle

Place the reins over the pony's head and check that there are no twists in them. The child should take a rein in each hand with the arms bent and the hands about 5 inches apart. Pass the rein between the little finger and the third finger, with the thumb holding the reins in position. The hands should have the palms upwards and the wrists should be flexible. (See Fig. 4.5.)

Having checked that the child's hands are correct, look again at her position in the saddle which has probably gone awry with concentration upon the new bridle. Her head should be up; shoulders back; legs vertical, from the knee downwards, with her feet under her body and her toes on the bar of the stirrups and pointing inwards. She should still be sitting well down in her saddle.

Telling the pony to walk on, lead your child quietly away and, as you walk her, tell her how she should give the pony

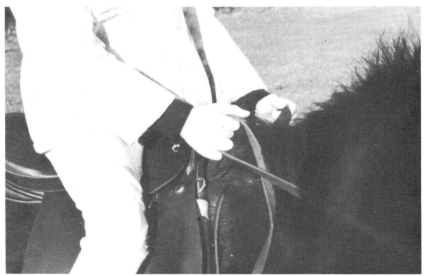

Fig. 4.5 Holding the reins.
The reins should be held between the correct fingers in a gentle manner without pulling on the pony's mouth.

(*Photo courtesy:* Susan Hulme)

the "aid" (or instruction) to walk on. She must use this once she has advanced to controlling her pony herself with the bridle. This may well be after one or two more half-hour sessions of this kind. Firstly, she should squeeze the reins very gently (**but never shake them**), and then apply her legs **gently** behind the girth; this is the signal for the pony to move off. As the pony begins to walk, she must immediately slacken the reins enough to allow the pony the freedom to move his head back and forth with his stride. Her hands should move with his head but always be in contact. Now you will understand why it is so important not to tax a small child with too many instructions at the start.

This walking instruction should be continued as often as possible. However, even after this advance, the neck strap should be left in place as a safeguard. If the child should lose her balance she may hold onto the neck strap instead of pulling the reins, thereby preventing the pony's mouth being jabbed.

LESSON FOUR

Once the child has learnt to hold the reins correctly she may progress to learning how to use them, together with her legs, in order to instruct the pony.

Walking and Halting

Whilst telling the pony to "Walk on" as before, get the child to tell him too, using her **hands, body and legs**. She should lean slightly forward, squeeze the reins gently, brush the pony behind the girths with her heels and then open her fingers enough to allow the pony his head so that he may move on. Now, keeping contact with his mouth in a gentle moving way as he moves his head back and forth, she will begin to feel that her pony is really obeying her, but Mother will still have hold of the leading rein and will be ready to assist if needed.

To halt, the child should say "**Whoa**" and exert a steady, even pull on the reins whilst inclining her body slightly backwards. At the same time, she should exert an even pressure on the pony's sides with her legs. In order to dismount, wait until the pony is still, tell your child to kick both feet out of the irons and, holding the reins in the left hand, bring the right leg over the pony's quarters and slide down with Mother to steady the landing.

LESSON FIVE

Once Daughter can cope with this walking and halting, she may progress to the **trot**. This need not be of very long duration and may be learnt at a walking pace initially.

The Trot

To do this, ask your child to lean a little forward in the saddle and, putting her weight on her irons, to raise her body a very small amount up from the saddle before sinking gently down again. There should be no jolt, as the spine naturally bends to prevent this, just as when you catch a cricket ball your hand sinks to receive it, thereby absorbing the landing of the ball. This movement should be repeated several times.

Now Daughter has an idea of what is required, Mother may lead the pony into a trot whilst still keeping level with his shoulder. You may find that counting aloud in time to the pony's "clip-clop" trot will help the rider to rise and sink in time with the rhythm of the counting which is also the rhythm of the pony. For example: "One-two, one-two, up-down, up-down". This is called **"posting"**.

LESSON SIX

The next lesson will be concerned with turning and, although the child will still be led, she will by now have some say in what the pony does and Mother will simply be there to avert any disaster.

Fig. 4.6 Progressing from the 'walk' (top) to the 'trot' (bottom). Mother should always be there to avert disaster.

(*Photos courtesy:* Susan Hulme)

Turning

To turn the pony you must use both your hands and your legs, as with most other actions. Your left hand should gently bend the pony's head to the left by moving out a fraction from the normal position thereby exerting a gentle pull on the left rein. At the same time your right hand should move a little forward to allow the bend of the neck to the left. Whilst using your hands as above, you should use your left leg to touch the girth in gentle taps whilst the right leg is left still behind the girth. Your body should follow the movements of the pony in much the same manner as it would if you were riding a bicycle. When turning right, all that has to be done is to reverse the above rules. Very soon, you and your pony will come to have such an understanding that he will turn when the opposite rein is laid on his neck. This is called "**neck reining**" and is a very useful accomplishment when riding in any sport which calls for one-handed steering, for example when taking part in games and gymkhanas, when one may be required to carry something.

LESSON SEVEN

The final lesson of our very elementary course for both Mother and Daughter in riding correctly from the start, is to sit at the canter. This may pose difficulties because few Mother's will be speedy enough on their own feet to run beside a cantering pony. The Author suggests that when this stage is reached, the help of a knowledgeable friend should be enlisted to lunge the pony. If the pony is well-schooled and quiet, the first canter may be tried whilst on the lungeing rein, with the neck strap still in position to give confidence. Whilst this lesson is taking place, preferably in an indoor school, but at any rate in a small fenced-off arena, Mother can learn just how to lunge correctly; a useful accomplishment when the daughter is away at school and the pony must be kept fit and quiet for her return.

Fig. 4.7 Using the lungeing rein.
This can be a very useful accomplishment when teaching the young rider to canter.

(*Photos courtesy:* Susan Hulme)

The Canter

The seat at the canter should be still from the waist down and the spine supple, rocking with the pony's one-two-three movement. The body should incline forward slightly and the hands should move with the pony's head, as at the walk. The legs should be close to the saddle, with the heels down and the toes in. The rider should be looking through her pony's ears, not downwards.

CAVALETTI

It is not within our scope to teach Mother and Daughter jumping, but the use of a few poles laid on the ground at intervals of about 4 feet will lay the foundation for more advanced work in the future. These poles may be walked over, trotted over and eventually cantered over. This will

Fig. 4.8 Jumping – cavaletti will lay the foundation for more advanced work in the future.

(*Courtesy:* K.G. Ettridge)

form a basis for work with **Cavaletti**, which is the next stage in the training of both pony and rider. Cavaletti are simply long round poles resting at each end on crossed pieces of wood.

Use of these poles will teach the pony to pick up his feet, to judge distance, and to keep a controlled and steady pace. They will also teach the novice the basic approach to jumping. You must learn to release his head as he approaches the jump and to keep him going straight, also to sit well down in the saddle at the canter and also when his stride becomes more definite as he times his steps to cope with the poles.

BENDING

A few bamboo sticks borrowed from the kitchen garden may be stuck into the ground at intervals and used for **Bending**, which means riding between the sticks in a snake-like path, without touching them. This should first be practised at a walk and, when proficient at this stage, they should then be taken at a trot and finally at a canter; the last pace being an excellent but much more advanced grounding for dressage later on, and not within the scope of this book. It is essential that this bending should be completely controlled and balanced. However, it is unfair to expect a green (un-schooled) pony to perform these movements at a canter and on grass. To do this perfectly would require the use of his hocks and the shifting of weight onto his quarters as he canters in a collected manner whilst leaning well into his bit. Therefore, at this stage, it is best to be content with walking and trotting when learning this new skill.

If your pony is well behaved and quiet, it may well come about that you will be asked to help out with him at a local centre of the "Riding for the Disabled" Group. If this opportunity arises, accept their invitation as this movement is doing untold good, both in re-habilitating those whose injuries are not permanent and helping those who have some permanent mental or physical handicap. As it usually takes three helpers to aid one handicapped rider, new volunteers are always welcome, as are quiet ponies.

CARE ON THE ROADS AND BRIDLEWAYS AND THE RIGHT TO RIDE ON THEM

There are now very few bridleways remaining for the use of the young rider and every parent of a riding child should do her utmost to help preserve those that are left to us. Even the country lanes are no longer safe from massive tankers and large agricultural machinery, complete with swaying fork-lifts. The less thought about the state of the roads themselves, the better; for riding on them hardly bears thinking about. Every year there are more reports of equestrian accidents, many of these being caused by drivers who apparently have no idea that horses do not run on wheels and, therefore, can leap out sideways as well as going backwards, upwards and, if the road is slippery, downwards too.

THE BRIDLEWAY

The law of bridleways is so intricate that it can have no place here. However, if one is riding down a green lane or bridleway and one comes to a new obstruction, then the correct procedure is to find out whether it is in fact a public bridleway. If this is so, then the next step is to report the matter to the local **Bridleways Association** representative, whose name and address can be ascertained from the district Pony Club Secretary.

It is legal to remove sufficient of the obstruction to make progress possible, or to make a diversion round the obstruction. The latter may be done only if the path *is* a bridleway and is shown as such on the definitive map. This

IN THE SADDLE

Fig. 4.9 Riding on the road — always thank motorists who show you consideration. Mother should lead the way and young children should not be allowed to ride unaccompanied.

map comes under review by the Parish Council, then the County Council and every five years there is a statutory revision.

THE ROAD

Riding on the road should be avoided whenever possible, especially if there is much traffic. Children attending Pony Club functions should make every effort to contact others with ponies and make arrangements to share a horse-box, rather than ride to the venue.

If riding a short distance on the road is inevitable, every precaution should be taken. The following are rules which should always be remembered and adhered to whenever possible:

1. Always ride close in to your side of the road.
2. Make use of the verge, when one is available, as this has the advantage of being less slippery and much safer to ride on than the road.
3. Slow down any fast-moving vehicles by steadily waving an arm up and down. This must be done in good time, in order that they may slow down before reaching you.
4. Stop cars approaching from behind from passing you if you are on a corner which you cannot see around or can see something approaching you, by the use of arm signals.
5. Always thank any motorist who shows you consideration.
6. Wear something white around your waist whenever you are riding in the dark, or at dusk.

Fig. 4.10 You can't catch me!
Most ponies will come to their owner when enticed with a titbit.
(*Photo courtesy:* Susan Hulme)

WHAT TO DO AND WHEN — SOME COMMON DIFFICULTIES AND HOW TO COPE WITH THEM

There are a number of standard problems likely to be encountered by the young rider in her first dealings with ponies. Here follows an account of some of the most common, together with suggestions as to how they may be overcome.

YOU CAN'T CATCH ME!

One of the most infuriating problems which may arise is that of the pony who will not be caught. To leave the head collar on and to attach a 10-inch strap to the ring underneath the throat may help, if it is simply a matter of the pony rushing off before you can get his head collar on. However, if he takes to galloping off to the other end of the field and moving on immediately you approach again, some other answer must be found.

Most ponies will follow their owner if she carries a pan with a morsel of food in it and it may be found best to appear in the pony's field, rattle the pan and call, and then walk away from him, still calling, towards the gate. If the stable or shed where you groom and tack him up is within his field, he will soon learn to follow you, and the food, inside. If you must put a head collar on him to lead him out of his field, stand to the side and slide the rope round his neck as he bends to eat his tit-bit, then put the head collar on and fasten it.

LEADING

Always walk on a level with the pony's shoulder when leading, never drag him behind you. If he does not move forward freely, give him a little tap with a short cane from behind your back, without turning round. If he moves off too fast, hold the cane in front of his nose saying "Steady".

To halt him say "Whoa" and when he halts on command, pat him and show him that you are pleased.

DIFFICULT PONIES

Some ponies which are used to trekking in a long line with other ponies, will not move forward alone and this problem may take an inexperienced rider a little time to sort out; it will need patience but it is not insoluble. Everything depends upon the calm determination of the rider to push the pony forward and so it is not a job for Mother and Daughter when only at the learning stage. However, it seldom happens that a pony will not even be led, for one person leading and another riding almost makes up to him for the loss of his companions and gives him confidence. Many ponies who shy and tend to be difficult when ridden alone will follow another child on a bicycle quite happily, trotting on when the cyclist accelerates and walking when he decreases his speed.

Fig. 4.11 Leading your pony.
Never drag your pony behind you when leading him.

This is a satisfactory arrangement for a start but the time will come when the pony must venture out alone, and this is probably when the help of an experienced and older rider will be needed if Daughter is only at the learning stage.

If the pony "naps" – refuses to go on – the rider should swing him round and round in a circle until he is so confused that he does not really know which way he is facing, is rather fed up, and so will then go on. The rider must keep him going forward and not allow him to stop until he is instructed to do so. It may then be made certain that the message is completely understood by making the pony go forward and away from home again.

The Author has several times found herself in possession of a pony which, all too often, had succeeded in whipping round and making for home when being ridden by her previous owner. In cases such as this, it is sometimes essential to alter the pony's bit. If a plain snaffle has been used, a Kimblewick may be found to give better control in keeping the pony straight. (See Fig. 2.4.)

GREED

Small children will not be able to keep their pony's head up if it persistently tries to graze. This is most frustrating for the child, who may even be pulled right out of the saddle and over the pony's head. To prevent this bad behaviour on the part of a greedy, small mount, tie a piece of cord to each ring of the bit, thread them up through the side-slots of the brow band, cross the two cords at the neck and finish by tying each to the "D" on the saddle. These cords must, of course, only restrict the pony enough to prevent its head reaching the grass.

SHYING

It must always be remembered that a shying pony is an unsafe one; for he may shy away from a bird flying out of a hedge or a paper blowing across the road and into something far more dangerous, like a passing car. However, a pony's tendency to shy may be only temporary and due to the fact that he is new to your part of the countryside where all the sights and sounds are strange to him.

The cure for this kind of nervousness is obviously to take him around until he has seen everything, whilst talking to him all the time in an encouraging manner. At first it would be wise to walk about with him, rather than lead him along with someone riding on his back. He should be allowed, in fact **encouraged**, to stop, look and smell anything which frightens him. One of the Author's ponies, who was persistently terrified of plastic or paper-feed bags, has been cured of shying by his young stable companion — a home-reared filly with no nerves. She tore up the bags and waved the pieces in her mouth, right under his nose! At first he was extremely alarmed, but she persisted and he has now learnt that they are what his food comes in and are nothing to be frightened of.

If your pony is frightened and shys away from water — paddle yourself, he will probably test the depth and follow you in. However, if he seems reluctant to cross a certain piece of ground, beware for he may have good reason; it may be boggy and if he is a mountain or moorland pony he will know more about bogs than you and will never risk the crossing. Therefore, when your pony shys, always consider his reasons for doing so, for he may have noticed something that you have missed and which could be a danger to both of you.

HOW TO DEAL WITH THE POSSESSIVE EATER

Some ponies and horses are very possessive about their feed buckets, and the Author has one which is downright dangerous if approached when feeding from her pan. This stemmed from an early mistake; her food was put in one corner of the stable where she was born, with her mother's bucket in the other. When one had finished she would race across to grab the other's, with the result that a kicking habit was formed.

The answer is to lead the pony in, turn her round to face the door and *then* remove the head collar and release her to eat. Her wish to eat alone should always be respected.

Fig. 5.1 Competing — what every young rider hopes to achieve: a clear round and that precious rosette.

CHAPTER 5

Going to a Show
BY MEG MASON — THE WOODBEER HIGHLAND PONY STUD

For the young rider who desires to enter the world of showing it is best to begin with the nearest small show. This may well be a gymkhana, and many of these include classes for "Mountain and Moorland Ponies", "Family Pony", "Best Turned out Pony and Rider" and "Best Rider". It is to the advantage of the learner if a start is made with these classes in order to gain experience. The "Fancy Dress" is a popular class and can be great fun so despite any misgivings, have a go.

ENTERING

You will find adverts for shows in your local paper, giving the name and address of the show secretary. Write and ask him for a schedule; this will give you a list of all the classes included in the show, the rules employed and a timetable of the events. Read the schedule right through, including the section on the rules. This may sound boring but it is terrible to enter a pony in a class and then be disqualified because of some rule you failed to read. For instance: most Mountain and Moorland (M & M) ponies must be shown in their natural state and usually no pulling of manes and tails, no trimming of heels or other changes are allowed. Plaiting-up is sometimes allowed in the M & M ridden classes but not in the "In-hand" classes.

CHOOSING YOUR CLASS

Next you must read again through the classes included, putting a pencil mark against those you would like to enter. Read the rules for each class carefully; make sure that you are the correct age and that your pony is the correct age and height. For the M & M classes he will need to be of a particular breed and have registration papers. You will have to copy his registered number onto the Entry Form for each show where he is competing in M & M classes. "Handy Pony", "Family Pony" and many other classes are for ordinary ponies with no pedigree papers, so there is usually plenty for everyone to do. There are often **In-hand** classes for young ponies. This means that you only lead your pony in the ring, he is not ridden. Even if you don't think that he is a super show type, this is a marvellous education for you and your pony and a good class in which to make your debut.

Check the timetable carefully to make sure that you are not trying to be in two places at once and then fill in your entry; a form for this purpose always comes with the schedule. Take care to write clearly and send the correct amount of money. Every show has a closing date for entries, so make sure that you do not dither about deciding which class to enter and then find that you have missed the closing date. It is a good idea to write the classes you have entered, their time and ring number on the front of your schedule, as this will save a lot of bother on the day.

PREPARATION FOR THE SHOW

There are many things to be taken into account when preparing for a show and, as all are of importance and vital if the show is to be problem-free, it is best to start preparations well-beforehand. The following is a list of considerations which, hopefully, will help any rider towards success on the day, especially if it is a "first-time".

TRANSPORT

Firstly one must think about transport to the show. If you can hack there or have your own method of transport, for example a horse box, then you have no problem to overcome. If you have to share hired transport, or hire it yourself, make sure that you contact the haulage firm six to eight weeks in advance and remember to remind the driver four or five days before the show of the time to collect you. Haulage firms are covered by insurance in case of accidents but if a friend gives you a lift, or you give a friend a lift, you will have to check up on the insurance cover.

WHAT TO WEAR ON THE DAY

Some people spend a lot of money on clothes for showing, whilst others turn out in old jeans and a dirty headscarf. The most important requirement, however, is to look clean and smart which can be achieved without extra expenditure on new clothes.

Clothing and tack requirements will vary according to which classes you have entered. The following is a brief guide to indicate what may be required by In-hand and Ridden classes.

Clothes for In-Hand Classes

Your usual riding kit, complete with riding hat, will be suitable when you are leading your pony. This outfit certainly looks very nice and instantly gives the judge a good impression. If, however, you find this outfit too warm or restricting when you are running your pony, then settle for the following: a pair of plain slacks, white shirt, plain jersey or hacking jacket (if the weather demands extra covering), tie and a neat, but unassuming, head covering. A neat headscarf will suffice for the latter, as long as it is not too flamboyant: you want the judge to look at your pony, not at your headscarf. A cap, deer stalker or man's porkpie hat, can also look neat. Many wear no hat but this leaves a slightly unfinished look about an outfit. Lastly, make sure that your shoes are clean.

Clothes for Ridden Classes

You will need a hacking jacket, jodhpurs, riding hat and either boots or shoes. Gloves are not essential but give a more finished look to an outfit. Do not worry about black coats, button holes and the like. Concentrate on being clean, neat and keeping your attire simple. Nothing is worse than an over-dressed mess.

A hacking cane should be carried by both In-Hand and Ridden classes. A neat ash stick can be cut from the hedgerow and is ample for a small show. At every show you will be required to wear a number on your arm or around your waist. This will be supplied by the show and should be collected from the secretary's tent as soon as you arrive. A good tip is to make yourself a band of brown (or whatever colour blends in with your jacket) elastic, with a hook on one end and a loop on the other. Make this the right size for your middle and then keep it in your coat pocket. When you get your number, use your elastic in place of the plastic string or whatever is supplied by the show. It will look neater and is easier to take off in between classes.

TACK

Tack for In-Hand Classes

It may be very nice to have a special In-Hand, brass-mounted bridle for shows, but unless many years of showing is intended it is as well to do with an ordinary leather head-collar for your very young pony. If this has brass buckles, then so much the better. To give the head collar a better appearance, wash it until it is spotless in warm, soapy water and then dry with a cloth. Leave for a day and then oil the underside and polish the top several times with brown shoe polish to give a good finish. A white leading rope with a spring clip can be made very smart by a good wash and an application of any shoe whitener.

A head collar and leading rope will suffice for a young pony but when showing an older pony an ordinary bridle may be used. The less fussy the bridle is, the better. Mountain and Moorland ponies should always be shown with a plain nose-band.

Tack for Ridden Classes

Use the bridle and bit which you normally use, as to borrow a double bridle will only confuse your pony and will, therefore, add nothing to your chances. Make sure that all your tack is spotless and avoid highly coloured girth straps; the same rule applies to these as to flamboyant headscarves.

WHAT TO TAKE ON THE DAY

Your pony, who is after all the star, must have the greatest possible amount of attention. This does not mean spending hours brushing, combing and cleaning, but it does mean having a plan, thinking ahead and making things easy by careful preparation. First of all sit down and make a list in a small and special note book. This should be kept in a particular place so that it can always be found when you need to add items which have been forgotten or that experience shows that you need. Begin by listing all the things you must wear and take on the day of the show; including hacking cane and money. Always remember to include a safety pin, aspirin and sticky plaster. Secondly, you must list all the things that your pony will need: his

Fig. 5.2 All set — pony and rider kitted out to compete in the Ridden classes.

(*Photo courtesy:* Susan Hulme)

tack, hay net, grooming kit and a bucket, in order that you may give him a drink. All shows provide water somewhere on the showground, but it may only be a tap. Lastly, remember to add the show schedule to the list, along with anything else that the secretary has sent you, as some shows send the competitors their numbers before the day.

Do not forget food and drink for yourself even if you think before-hand that you will not be needing any — almost certainly you will.

If your list is complete, then it will be invaluable to you on the day, when your nerves might otherwise cause you to forget something really important. Once you have assembled everything in list form, you can then forget about it and carry on with thinking about your pony.

PREPARING YOUR PONY FOR A SHOW

Preparation for any type of showing begins a long time before the show itself and differs according to the classes entered. The following should serve as a basic guide to training for In-hand and Ridden classes.

IN-HAND CLASSES

If you are going to begin with a young pony in the In-Hand classes, then you must begin at least six weeks before show day to teach your pony to lead correctly, stand properly and to run out well. It is as well to teach your pony to obey words of command such as "Woah", "Walk-on", "Trot-up" and "Stand". In an In-Hand class you will be required to lead your pony round the ring with all the other competitors, probably in a clockwise direction to begin with and often anti-clockwise as well. Give yourself plenty of room. **Do not** go in first with a young pony, follow someone else; about third or fourth is a good position. If you tend to catch up with the pony in front, walk round in a larger circle or, if that is not possible, turn around on the spot in a small circle. To keep stopping will unsettle your pony.

When you are called into line in the centre of the ring, stand your pony nicely and try to keep him calm by talking to him. However, you must remember to keep an eye on what is going on. **Do not** talk to other competitors or to friends around the ring, you must concentrate absolutely on showing your pony to the exclusion of everything else. Whilst training at home, lead your pony in a field one day and on the road the next, thereby giving him variety, for it is most important that he does not get bored. You can practise standing still even on the road; begin with small stops and be content with standing for only a few seconds. Gradually you may lengthen the time of standing. Always praise your pony when he responds correctly to your commands.

Next in the show you will be required to run your pony out for the judge. Always be prepared as nothing irritates a

Fig. 5.3 Pony ready to compete in an In-hand class.
(*Owner:* Mrs Blake, *photo courtesy:* Charles Curtis)

GOING TO A SHOW

judge more than a long pause while you collect your wits, drop your stick and trip over the inevitable mole hill! Lead your pony up to the judge and stand him so that he can be inspected, then stand in front of him. You should have a nut in your pocket just for this moment; keep it in your hand and let the pony smell it to keep him interested while the judge sizes him up.

You may be asked how old your pony is before you are asked to walk away from the judge and trot back. This you must practise at home, with a friend to act as judge. Your pony must walk away in a straight line, turn quietly, with you turning round your pony, then walk three steps forward in order to get straight again before you ask him to "Trot up". He should then trot straight at the judge, who will step aside for you to pass after he has seen how your pony moves, and continue at a trot around the line of ponies until your original place is reached. Walk the last

Fig. 5.4 Fun and games for all — there are many classes to enter at the average show. *(Courtesy:* K.G. Ettridge)

few yards and stand your pony again. **Now** and only now give him the nut you have hidden in your hand. An important thing to remember as you stand in the line is not to relax. At any moment the judge may glance back at your pony to compare him with the one being currently judged. Therefore, you must not be caught with your pony fast asleep and looking at his worst. This applies until the moment when you finally leave the ring.

After the judge has looked at everyone in turn, you will all be asked to walk around again before the final choice is made. You will then be lined up in the order of merit. If you are lucky and have won a rosette, tie it on the pony's bridle on the near side so that as you parade around the audience can see who won what. If you were not lucky, try to look pleasant even if you feel depressed; there are plenty more shows in which you can take part and the important thing is to make sure that you gain experience and improve with each outing.

One other thing to practise at home is fixing on a rosette. Any piece of fluttery ribbon will do, but some ponies object at first to having an adornment tied on their bridle and must be used to this before their first show.

RIDDEN CLASSES

For all the Ridden classes the In-Hand drill applies, but you must add to your practising. In the Ridden class you will be asked to give an individual show. This **must** be practised at home. You must be able to walk, trot and then canter; if your pony is over 12.2 h.h. you will be expected to demonstrate a short gallop. Mark out a place about the size of two tennis courts, end to end, and in that sort of area practise walking away down one side, trotting across the short end and then cantering diagonally across the whole area. On reaching the far end turn on the other rein and return to a trot until you reach the corner again. Once more turn across the diagonal into a canter, keeping at this

Fig. 5.5 Concentration — with practise and experience Daughter will soon be competing in gymkhana events.
(*Courtesy:* K.G. Ettridge)

pace as you turn across the short end. Now when you turn down the long side, sit down in your saddle and push your pony into a short gallop. This need only be for a few strides and then you may return to a canter. Continue around the whole area, before returning to a trot and finally a walk. You should now be back in the place where you began your walk. Halt and count to three slowly, then smile at the judge to thank him for watching you and return to your place. Remember that, as in the In-Hand class, the judge may suddenly look back at you again, so sit up and sit still and watch what goes on. Criticise all the other performers in your mind and learn from them.

"Working Pony" and "Handy Pony" classes are rather more involved and it would be just as well not to make your debut in one of these, or in gymkhana events. These can be tremendous fun when both you and your pony are used to the show ring, but they are not really a good way to begin.

THE SMART PONY

You know what you are going to do, what you will be wearing and how your pony should behave. How then, should he be presented on show day?

Again preparation should be made well in advance. Do not try to show your pony until he is in his summer coat which will usually be about the second week in May. As his winter coat begins to fall, give him a good scrape each day with a *rubber* Curry comb followed by a Dandy brush, as this will assist the shedding of the old hair, (a good fast ride, making the pony sweat, followed by a good currying when he is dry will often help). When his winter coat is almost out, this treatment will be too severe and you must then use a Body brush which is softer.

Ponies' manes and tails are a problem as too much brushing and combing breaks off the hair and ruins a good full mane or tail. Therefore, the mane and tail should be combed through very carefully and then washed in soap flakes or a hair shampoo. **Do not use a detergent** which will dry all the grease and make the hair very brittle. Thereafter, brush the mane and tail out with a very old and soft Dandy or Body brush; often a dog brush can be found that is ideal. White tails which are very stained have to be washed every day for ten days or more to get them white. The best method is to use a bar of plain household soap, clamp the tail, rub in the soap, rinse and repeat. A final rinse in Reckets Blue will help.

It is best to keep your pony in a stable the night before the show, as he is less likely to appear soaking wet and covered in mud when you go to catch him in the morning. However, if you are going to stable him it should be done for at least

Fig. 5.6 The Smart Pony.

(*Courtesy:* K.G. Ettridge)

three nights before the show, for a complete change of routine and diet (because he will have to have a feed of hay when in at night) may upset him completely and all you will have on show day is a pony with colic, or one who is all sweated up through being kept in. If you can keep him in overnight, he must be bedded down well; sawdust is the best bedding for keeping a pony clean.

The day before the show everything should be ready and your list ticked off. **Do not practise at all with your pony on the last day**. Shampoo him all over in the morning, using a pony shampoo or soap flakes. Make sure that you rinse him thoroughly and rub him well all over with an old towel whilst putting another big, bath towel over his back, before walking him quietly until he is dry. Once he is dry, he should be returned to his stable and given some hay. Unless your pony is to go outside again, you should brush out his mane and tail, put the whole tail in a nylon stocking and bandage it over the top with a stretchy tail bandage. If your pony has to go out again, make sure he has a feed of hay and goes out only when the sun is still shining. On no account should a damp pony be turned out as night is falling, as he will catch a chill, or worse. A feed of hay or nuts will warm him up.

In the morning get up extra early and bring your pony in or, if he is in, feed him and tidy his stable. Brush him over lightly, remove the tail bandage and leave him in peace to have his food whilst you have a good breakfast yourself. After this, give your pony a good groom, oil his hooves and put on his tail bandage again. You are now ready to leave.

AT THE SHOW

Make sure that you reach the show at least half an hour before your class begins. Collect your number, dress yourself, get your pony out of the horse-box, if he is in one, remove the tail bandage and give him a final brush over. If you have to change his head collar for a bridle it is as well to do this before you take him out of the box.

After your classes are over, see that your pony has a drink and is safe and comfortable in his horse box before you go off to watch other classes or walk around the stalls that many shows have. There is always plenty to see even at a small show. Even if you do not win a rosette, have a real day out. Look, learn, be entertained and make it a day to remember with pleasure.

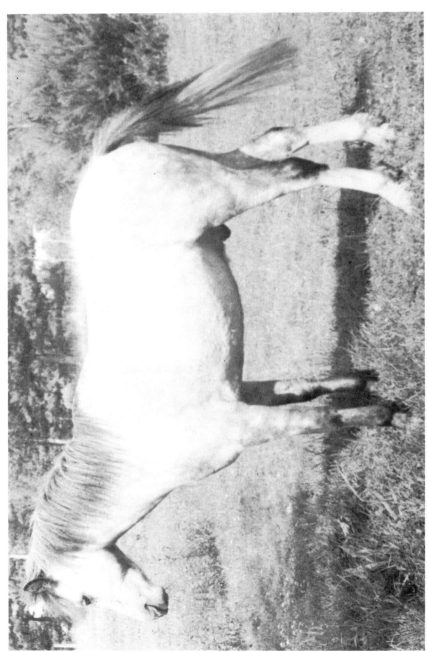

Fig. 6.1 New Forest pony in his natural surroundings.

CHAPTER 6

The Breeds

THE NEW FOREST PONY

The New Forest Pony's natural habitat is that part of the land which lies between Southampton and Bournemouth and this has been their home for many hundreds of years; to quote the Breed Society's own history of their breed "Canute's Forest Law of 1016 records the presence of horses among the other wild animals of the Forest". Arab and Thoroughbred blood is said to have been introduced somewhat indiscriminately into the New Forest breed from time to time, but this was prevented after 1891 when the **Society for the Improvement of New Forest Ponies** was founded, followed by the **Burley and District New Forest Pony and Cattle Breeding Society** in 1906. In 1938 these two societies amalgamated, in order that they could work together for the good of the breed.

Today there are many studs outside the Forest, and indeed, these have spread to cover almost the entire world, as is the case with most of our Native breeds. To buy a New Forest Pony one may attend one of the **Beaulieu Road sales**, which are held six times annually; catalogues may be obtained from T. Ensor and Sons, Dorchester, who are the auctioneers. The better plan for the new owner, however, is to write direct to the Breed Society which maintains a list of ponies for sale and will give intending purchasers every assistance. (See Chapter 8 for the addresses of all Breed Societies.)

These ponies should not be worked until they are three years of age, preferably not until they reach four, and should be kept in their natural habitat as far as this is possible. Good outdoor conditions are essential and the pony should have a shed, plenty of hay in winter and good grazing with windbreaks in the field.

This breed is docile, hardy, easy to teach and good in traffic, which it has seen and been used to since its first days, being forest bred. The New Forest is usually a good driving pony, an able jumper, fast, and an easy breeder. The larger ponies can carry a light adult, the smaller are of good quality and of a narrow build which is suitable for the younger rider.

Fig. 6.2 New Forest pony — *Peveril Taylor Maid*.
(*Owner/breeder:* Mrs P.B. Haycock)

Breed Standards

Height: No lowest height limit, maximum 14.2 h.h.
Colours: Any colour except piebald, skewbald or blue-eyed cream; bays and browns predominate; white markings on head and legs permitted.
Type: Riding type, with substance.
Head: Pony head, well-set.
Shoulders: Sloping.
Quarters: Strong.
Bone: Strong and plenteous.
Body: Deep.
Feet: Hard and round.
Action: Free, active and straight, but not exaggerated.

THE HIGHLAND PONY

The Highland is one of our largest and strongest Native ponies, and there is no doubt that he will carry Father, as well as Mother and older child. They range in height from 13 h.h. to 14.2 h.h. high but even the smaller sized ponies, having the true riding shoulder, can carry more weight than most other ponies of similar height.

In the Highlands there is absolutely no job which they can not be called upon to perform; carrying stags down to the road from the stalkers on the hill, hauling timber, carrying shepherds and farmers, pony trekking and driving. In character they are extremely intelligent, docile, willing and, on rough ground, very sure-footed. It would be well nigh impossible to ride a Highland pony into a bog, as their sense of safety regarding the nature of the land is acute.

In their native hills they find shelter on the lee side but in the south, where the fields may be flat and have little shelter, they seem to feel the cold more and will gladly take

Fig. 6.3 Highland stallion—*Glenhaylmer* (*Owner:* Mr. Hugh McGregor & Son)

advantage of an open shed in very wet weather. The hair is of two kinds: a strong outer covering with a softer, woolly undercoat, so that cold without wet does them little harm. Highland ponies jump well and in treacherous country where speed counts for little, they make excellent hunters.

The breeding of Highlands can be a very successful business. A Highland mare put with a Thoroughbred stallion and the resultant progeny bred with either another Thoroughbred stallion or an Arabian, will result in a fine offspring. As this is a very good line of breeding if an eventer of high class and sagacity is desired, many well-known and extremely successful horses have one quarter Highland blood.

Breed Standards

Colours: Various shades of dun: mouse, yellow, golden, grey, cream and fox are accepted. Also

Fig. 6.4 Highland pony — *Jaunty Laddie of Manshay.*
(*Courtesy:* The Woodbeer Stud)

grey, brown, black and occasionally bay and liver chestnut, with a silver mane and tail.

Most ponies carry the dorsal eelstripe and many have zebra markings on the inside of the foreleg.

Apart from a small star, white markings such as blazes and socks are disliked and discouraged. Ponies presented for Appendix registration with white markings will no longer be accepted.

Head: Well carried; broad between alert and kindly eyes; short between eyes and muzzle; muzzle not pinched; nostrils wide

Shoulders: Well laid back; withers pronounced

Quarters: Powerful, strong; well developed thigh and second thigh.

Body: Compact; back has slight natural curve; deep chest; ribs: well sprung and carried well back.

Feet: Hooves: well shaped, hard and dark.

Legs: Flat, hard bone; forearm: strong and well-placed under weight of body; broad knee; short cannon; pasterns: oblique and not too short; hocks: clean, flat and closely set; feathers: silky and not over heavy, ending in a prominent tuft at the fetlock.

Neck: Strong and not too short; good arched topline; throat clean and not fleshy.

THE DARTMOOR PONY

Being one of the smaller ponies, this breed is excellent for the younger child and is very hardy, having existed on the heights of Dartmoor for centuries. Those which were in any way sub-standard physically could not have survived, so that only the fittest lived to breed, and rear stock unsurpassed for vigour and endurance. This little pony is of true

Fig. 6.5 Dartmoor ponies. (Bred by Wing Cmdr. Passey)
Left: *Blachford Impact* Right: *Blachford Brandween*

riding type and mares can be used to advantage with small Thoroughbred stallions, or with Arabian stallions, to produce a larger pony, of great quality.

Breed Standards

Height: Not to exceed 12.2 h.h.
Colours: Bay, black, or brown preferred; no colour barred except for skewbalds and piebalds; excessive white to be discouraged.
Type: Riding.
Head: Small and well set.
Ears: Very small and alert.
Neck: Strong, but not too heavy; should be neither long nor short.
Body and Quarters: Strong and well covered with muscle.
Feet: Tough and well shaped.
Tail: Set high and full.
Action: Low, free, typical hack or riding action.

THE CONNEMARA PONY

This beautiful and ancient breed of ponies comes from the region of Western Galway in Ireland and in their native environment, one of considerable hardship, they usually grow to about 13.2 h.h. However, when reared under more favourable conditions, with good food and better grazing and perhaps some shelter at night during winter, they will grow to about 14 to 14.2 h.h. Faster than the Highland, although not up to carrying such great weights, it is said that the Connemara contains Arab blood. This combined with its staying powers, tremendous activity and kindly temperament makes it one of the wisest choices for the more advanced child who wishes to compete, and also for Mothers who hunt.

Fig. 6.6 Connemara pony. (*Courtesy*: Susan Hulme)

Breed Standards

Height:	13.2 to 14.2 h.h.
Colours:	Grey, black, brown, dun, and occasional roans and chestnuts are accepted; the predominant colour is grey; the yellow dun is not so common as it was.
Type:	Riding.
Bone:	Clean, hard and flat, measuring approximately 7 to 8 inches below the knee.
Head:	Well balanced head and neck.
Body:	Compact and deep, standing on short legs.
Action:	Free, easy and true movement.

WELSH PONIES AND COBS

There are four types of pony, each differing from the others in a variety of ways, but all four types of pony and cob have the Welsh Mountain Pony as their common ancestor, and this may well be the reason for the tremendous hardiness and strength of them all. It is this strength, combined with their great beauty, which makes them much in demand, not only as pure bred Welsh, but for crossing with other breeds and with the Thoroughbred. All four types are driven as well as ridden, all jump well and all can be found in many other parts of the world. The larger ponies and cobs are, like the Highland, the Dales and the Fell ponies, much in demand for trekking, as they combine great weight-carrying ability with sure-footedness and an equable temperament.

During the war years, the Author owned a Welsh cob which ploughed her land, cut her hay, cultivated, carted, shopped (pulling a milk float), and was not by any means at the tail end of the hunting field on his days off. He never spent a night indoors in all his twenty-seven years.

THE BREEDS

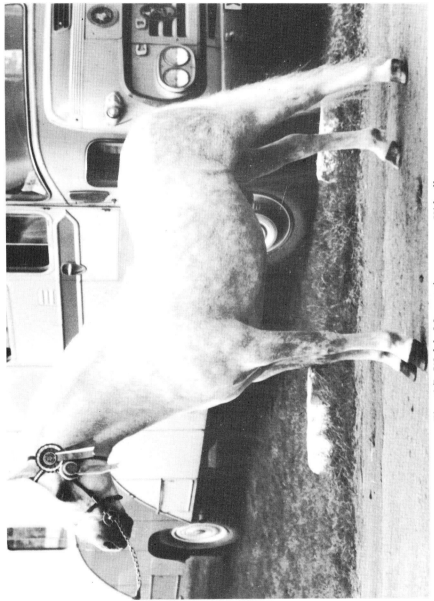

Fig. 5.7 Welsh Mountain pony — *Kidwell*.
(*Courtesy*: The Rosedale Stud, *photo courtesy*: Creighton Graphics)

SECTION A — THE WELSH MOUNTAIN PONY

Breed Standards

Height:	Not to exceed 12 h.h.
Colour:	Any colour accepted except piebald and skewbald.
Head:	Small, with neat pointed ears, big bold eyes and wide forehead.
Jaw:	Clean-cut with small muzzle; silouette concave or dished, but never convex or too straight.
Neck:	Of good length, well-carried shoulders sloping back to well defined wither.
Legs and Feet:	Squarely set, good flat bone.
Tail:	Set high and gaily carried.
Action:	Straight both in front and behind; quick and free with hocks well flexed

SECTION B — WELSH PONY OF RIDING TYPE

Height: Not to exceed 13.2 h.h.

The description of the Welsh Mountain above fits the Section B pony, with greater emphasis upon the fact that this type was used by hill farmers for herding and, in consequence, was required to carry a full grown man over difficult terrain.

SECTION C — THE WELSH PONY OF COB TYPE

This pony is a stronger example with Cob blood, and is ideal for the older child and for Mother too. An excellent ride and drive pony. Height not to exceed 13.2 h.h.

SECTION D — THE WELSH COB

Height: Exceeding 13.2 h.h.

The largest and strongest of the Welsh family, greatly in demand overseas and having great success in the international driving world.

THE BREEDS

Fig. 6.8 Welsh pony yearling filly — *Millcroft Desiree*.
(*Owner/Breeders*: Mr. & Mrs. John Carter, *photo courtesy*: Judy Meakin)

Breed Standards

Head: Great quality combined with pony character; bold prominent eyes; broad forehead; neat, well-set ears.

Body: Deep, strong; well-ribbed

Legs: Good hard-wearing joints; plenty of bone

Action: Straight, free and forceful; the knees should be bent and then the whole foreleg extended from the shoulders as far as possible, in all paces.
The hocks should be well-flexed with powerful leverage.

THE DALES PONY

The Dales pony grows up to 14.2 h.h. and is a strong, sound, free-moving pony of character and substance. They are usually black in colour, although there are some bays and browns and an occasional grey.

In their home environment — the North Riding of Yorkshire, Northumberland and Durham — they have been bred for very many years on the hills of the Northern Dales farms and have been used for all farm work, shepherding and driving and originally were also used as pack ponies by the mines. They are extremely hardy and can stand very cold conditions, as well as being economical to keep. Since the advent of pony trekking they have, like the Highland and the other larger Native ponies, proved their worth and ability to carry considerable weights for long days over rough hilly tracks.

A Dales mare put to a Thoroughbred stallion produces a weight-carrying cob, or a hunter with substance.

Breed Standards

Height: Up to 14.2 h.h.

THE BREEDS

Colour: Black predominating.
Head: Wide across the eyes which should be bright and docile
Muzzle of medium width; intelligent, alert expression.
Ears: Medium sized and erect.
Shoulders: Deep, sloping and well-laid in.
Quarters: Hindquarters balanced and compact.
Body: Deep girth with great heart room; well-sprung rib
Back: Short and strong.
Legs: Forearm: straight, flat-boned and tapering to knee; cannon bone: short and straight; hocks: broad, strong and clean-cut; feathers should be straight and silky.
Feet: Broad, hard and blue in colour.
Action: Clean and straight.

Fig. 6.9 Welsh cob — *Llanarth Meredith.*
(Owned and bred by the Llanarth Stud)

Fig. 6.10 Dales pony. *(Courtesy:* Mrs. P. Fitzgerald)

THE EXMOOR PONY

Height: Should not exceed 130 cm.

The ponies of Exmoor are said to have roamed these Moors for centuries and have a similar ancestry to the Dartmoor breed of pony. Certainly they have quite distinctive attributes, being very active and strong with great powers of endurance and, having run for many years over these rough and wild moors, are amazingly sure-footed. They make excellent children's ponies being sweet-tempered, alert and of good quality.

Their coat is harsh and springy in winter, shiny and sleek in summer. The most common colour is brown, though grey and bay are also seen. One of their most distinctive characteristics is a mealy-coloured muzzle.

THE FELL PONY

It is nearly eighty years since the Fell ponies worked at their original labour which was carrying lead from the mines to the docks on Tyneside. Twenty ponies, accompanied by one mounted man, walked one behind the other, carrying a load of 16 stone of lead in panniers, 8 stone on each side. Each week these ponies walked some 240 miles and it seems that the Dale ponies were normally amongst them, for eighty years ago the two breeds intermingled.

Wild, high, and, in winter, bitterly cold moorland and mountain is their native heath and they are, therefore, extremely hardy, sure-footed and sensible. They are an excellent ride-and-drive pony and can also carry a considerable weight.

Breed Standards

Height: Should not exceed 14 h.h.
Colours: As above.
Head: Pony type; sharp, well-placed ears.

Fig. 6.11 Exmoor winners.
(*Owner:* Mrs. W. Vint, *photo courtesy:* Judy Meakin)

Fig. 6.12 Fell Pony.
(*Photo courtesy:* Fell Pony Society)

Shoulders:	Long and sloping, well laid back; neck of reasonable length with well defined crest.
Quarters:	Generous, strong and muscular.
Body:	Again very strong and muscular; girth measurement should be about 6 feet.
Legs:	Squarely set; well-developed, prominent knees; hocks: wide apart, large, clean and parallel with the body, excellent bone; heels abundantly feathered.
Mane and Tail:	Very long and silky; tail set fairly high and gaily carried.

THE SHETLAND

This is the smallest of all our Native breeds being very hardy and strong due to the hard climate of their windswept native islands. Although their height is suitable for a small child, their build is such that they are often too wide, which can only lead to an uncomfortable and unsafe ride.

Shetlands have great intelligence and a determined temperament; unfortunately, as has been said, some are distinctly self-willed and, for this reason, the Author feels they are not a suitable pony for the young rider.

Fig. 7.1 Two three-day old Welsh fillies.

CHAPTER 7

A Foal?

Although breeding information is not really included in this book, it is a great pleasure to breed and rear a foal from the child's pony and it may well happen that the pony would otherwise be idle for a time, perhaps because her young owner is away at school, or studying for exams. A first pony which is outgrown, but which is so loved that no-one in the family can bear the thought of parting with her, can also earn her keep in this way.

It may be of interest to note that a famous point-to-point rider in the West Country bred her horses from her own child's pony, by persistent mating with a Thoroughbred. By the time this lady was in her thirties she had achieved her ambition to breed, break, train and race her own winner.

Although mares are always said to be more unpredictable in their behaviour than geldings (castrated males), they are more affectionate and quicker in the uptake, and for the reasons already given, the Author would always prefer to buy a mare. The choice of a stallion must depend upon the individual circumstances, and reference to the chapters on the Native breeds is suggested. There is also the possibility of having a larger pony covered by a small Thoroughbred riding pony, thus breeding a mount likely to suit the older girl in her more advanced and ambitious stages. Having decided upon the breed of stallion, the Breed Society secretary may be approached for information about studs.

A mare takes eleven months to produce her foal and it is usually best for the foal to be born in April or May, for she will then have the benefit of the early spring grass and will miss the worst of the winter. The mare may be taken to a stud and left to run with the stallion chosen, or she may be served and brought straight home, according to the stud's management. However, it is wise to book, even though the pony may not show obvious signs of being in season, and may have to be left. A charge is usually made for keep, together with a couple of pounds for the groom and then on top of this there is the stud fee, which is unlikely to be more than £50 for a pony mare.

MANAGEMENT OF THE IN-FOAL MARE

For the first five months no very great change needs to be made in the pony's management and she may be ridden quietly. As the value goes out of the grass with the onset of autumn, some supplementary feeding will be needed apart from hay. This may take the form of well-soaked sugar beet pulp given with bran for one feed (refer to Chapter 2 on feeding), and some pony nuts and bran for a second feed. Alternatives are bran given with grass nuts, diced carrots and bran mashes.

By the time that the pony mare is eight months in-foal, she should begin to have stud nuts instead of pony nuts in her rations and her hay should be of the very best quality and should smell so delicious that you could almost eat it yourself. At this time of year the grass will be almost valueless and hay will be the most important item in her diet.

The following diet will be sufficient for an in-foal pony mare of about 13.2 h.h. and should be given apart from good quality hay which must be available at all times. The

A FOAL?

mare should be given about 2 lb of stud nuts together with 1 lb of damped broad bran twice a day. An extra feed may be given at mid-day in the form of about 8 oz (dry weight) of well-scalded, soaked sugar beet pulp and broad bran. A feed of 2 lb of diced carrots dusted with bran makes a good alternative to the latter. A Rockie salt-lick may be supplemented by a good pinch of Equivite in each of the above feeds. Drinking water must be available to the little mare at all times; it must be clean, fresh and not frozen.

Her shoes should be removed at about this time, but it is important to remember that her feet will need trimming at least every two months.

FOALING

When foaling time draws near, be prepared to forgo the pleasure of actually seeing the foal born. Mares do not like

Fig. 7.2 Mother and Daughter.

(Photo courtesy: Jane Miller)

to be observed, so it is best if she is kept in a safe field with no dangerous places and, keeping your distance, check from time to time that all is well. Mares usually foal very quickly once labour begins and are to be found standing up within thirty minutes of foaling, encouraging the foal to get to its feet. If the mare does not rise within thirty minutes, there must be some reason and a vet may be needed. As soon as the foal is up and has suckled, its mother will probably take it for a trial run round the field. Therefore, it is important that the little animal does not fall into any deep ditches or run into wire which it may not see very well at first. The Author has found that by the time the foals are a few days old, they have learnt to respect the electric fence which is a lesson they never forget, and one which becomes invaluable if one wants to strip-graze a field instead of utilising the whole at once, as this can be wasteful. It is also important to remember that later, when the flies begin to be a pest, both mare and foal will require shelter at mid-day and this must be provided for.

MANAGEMENT OF THE FOAL

When the foal is about three days old, have both mother and child indoors and put a foal slip on the foal. It may then begin lessons in being led about behind its mother before it becomes strong. Once it has learnt to come when called and to be led, it is half-way to being a civilized little animal. There will be fewer problems later on than there may be with a bought-in pony, for yours will have learnt that you are its friend but that you mean what you say, so from an early age you will have gained both its respect and affection.

FEEDING

Foals, particularly Native pony foals, begin to graze when a few hours old, and very soon it will need its own pan of feed which should contain a little of what the mare is having. By this time the grass should be at its best, so very little else will be required by either mare or foal if the mare is milking well. However, the Author always has both in twice a day for a tiny feed of bran with a good pinch of Equivite, simply to check on them and see that all is well. If a hay net is used, be very careful that it is well out of reach of the foal's feet, or a nasty accident could happen.

The time will arrive when there will be a certain amount of competition over the feeds and it will be best for both if one is fed inside the stable and one outside or, if no stable is available, one fed on each side of the gate. A bad habit of kicking when fed is easily acquired and not easily stopped.

Opinions differ as to the best age to wean the foal but, since nothing is better for it than its mother's own milk, it should have the benefit, for at least six months, of all that it can take. If the mare is covered again and is in-foal, she may

Fig. 7.3 Contentment.
(*Courtesy:* Mrs P. Blake, *photo courtesy:* Jane Miller)

discourage her first born and wean it when she thinks that she must build herself up for the next one. If not, the foal may have to be found a companion of its own age to run with, away from and out of sight and hearing of the mare.

A colt foal is usually castrated at about six months, but early castration of a large and strong foal may be deemed wise and on this matter you should consult the veterinary surgeon.

Fig. 7.4 Welsh colt foal.

(*Courtesy:* K.G. Ettridge)

CHAPTER 8

Societies and Clubs

THE PONY CLUB

The Pony Club, which was started soon after the Author left school and was, in consequence, of no help personally, began in 1929 as a very valuable offspring of the **Institute of the Horse**. The first Pony Club branches included that of the Old Surrey and Burstow Hunt, already famous for its follower Mr. Jorrocks!

Soon nearly every Hunt had its Pony Club branch, and evidence of the wonderful work which it had begun to carry out could clearly be seen in the names of those famous early show-jumping members as they grew up and went on to find fame and fortune. Almost all of the great names in jumping and eventing were earlier to be found in some branch of the Pony Club.

Once the child has become confident and comfortable in the saddle, and is no longer a mere passenger, she may, with very great advantage, join her local branch and progress under their excellent teaching to more advanced riding. Here she will meet other children with the same interests, ride other ponies (and this is of great importance), and, it is only fair to give due warning, Mother will probably find herself allocated some job to do. By virtue of three Pony Club daughters, the Author's own niece has been a District Commissioner for many years.

Fig. 8.1 Pony Club meeting — an excellent way to meet other young riders and their ponies.

For information on joining Pony Club Camps and local branches, write to:–

> The Pony Club,
> The National Equestrian Centre,
> Stoneleigh,
> Warwicks.

Useful publications to help the young rider are the Pony Club manuals and the A, B and C tests.

THE NATIONAL PONY SOCIETY

The National Pony Society does a splendid job for all the Native breeds of pony and will be found most helpful. An excellent booklet is published by this group, giving information on all the activities of the Breed Societies, as well as those of the parent body.

The National Pony Society administers the grant given by the Horse Race Betting Levy Board, holds an annual two-day show, two annual sales and co-operates with everyone working for the welfare of ponies. There are Diploma schemes and various examinations in which varied qualifications may be gained.

The address of the Secretary is:–

> National Pony Society,
> 7, Cross and Pillory Lane,
> Alton,
> Hampshire.

SECRETARIES OF THE NATIVE PONY BREED SOCIETIES

English Connemara Society:
Miss S. Hodgkins,
Buttermilk Farm,
Leafield, Oxford

Fell Pony Society:
Miss P. Crossland
Packway,
Windemere,
Cumbria

Fig. 8.2 At a Pony Club Gymkhana.
(*Courtesy*: K.G. Ettridge)

Fig. 8.3 Fell ponies enacting 'The Border Reevers' — another Pony Club activity.

The Dartmoor Pony Society:
Mrs. E.C.M. Williamson,
Weston Manor,
Corscombe, Dorset

Exmoor Pony Society:
Mrs. J. Watts,
Quarry Cottage,
Sampford Brett, Williton,
Somerset

Highland Pony Society:
Mrs. J.M. Thomson,
Wester Sunnyside,
Nr. Methven,
Perthshire PH1 3RF

Dales Pony Society:
Mr. G.H. Hodgson,
Ivy House Farm,
Hilton,
Yarm-on-Tees, Yorkshire

New Forest Pony Society:
Miss D.M. MacNair,
Beacon Corner, Burley,
Ringwood, Hampshire

The Welsh Pony & Cob Society:
T.E. Roberts, Esq.,
6, Chalybeate Street,
Aberystwyth,
Dyfed SY23 1HS
Wales